THE

STRAINS

OF

WAR

A TRUE STORY AND STILL GROWING...

BY

R. GAGE AMSLER

Book Layout & Design by PIXEL eMarketing INC.

ISBN-13: 978-1514259696

Legal Disclaimer

DEDICATED TO...

My loving daughter Sophia;

Roseanna and Carmen for their support;

All veterans and contractors alike that served/worked in the war and all those suffering from PTSD and their families and friends that so strongly support them, and anyone else that may be suffering in silence; Task Force Team DragonSlayer; and Brian "Hershey" Reese R.I.P.

CONTENTS

A SOLDIER'S HEART

"Don't criticize a snake for not having a horn;
for all you know it may someday become a dragon."
UNKNOWN

I was born Robert Floyd Amsler Jr., but nobody ever knew me by that name. After my father split, I moved to Michigan with my grandparents and adopted a new one: Gage.

My grandfather was an easy man to admire. He told us ghost stories about a family that lived in his house before him. There was one young man who looked like me: a smart, decent man who spent his life doing good things for other people. I liked his story and decided that his name suited me better than the one my father had given me. The day I made that decision, my grandfather never called me anything but Gage.

In later years, my team would come to know me as "Doc." I did not know it back then when I was still being raised, but I had always had a heart for service, a soldier's heart. It took me a long time to come to terms with this calling, and I still have nights when I close my eyes and struggle to breathe from the weight of it all.

For a long time my service as a paramedic, a fire fighter, and a soldier robbed me of the ability to accept the world as it is. I found myself steeped in contradictions, part of an ongoing internal battle that made no sense and could not be won. Once you have been in the thick of war, something sticks to you. No normal situation ever feels that way again.

I know a lot of good men who have served and fallen—not to enemy fire or heroically on a remote mountaintop somewhere in the Middle East but to the ceaseless impact of PTSD. It affects us all. No one ever sets out prepared for these internal battles. Fresh-faced and idealistic, becoming a soldier nearly always starts from a place of love and service.

Then war seeps in. What began as a great way to get qualified, to support your family, and to serve your country becomes the reason why you can never return home. War changes men, and once you have seen its true nature, you can never un-see it. And so soldiers return home haunted by ghosts of memories past.

I was no different. There were times when these ghosts threatened to swallow me whole. Then I discovered something by accident one day on a routine mission: a plant that I had heard so much about. This discovery saved my life. This book takes you through that story as best as I can tell it. There was a sense of divine providence that day.

So here I am putting the words down. I am not afraid of who I am anymore, and I want other soldiers to find their way out of the darkness too. There is a path that leads back home. It is not widely accepted just yet, and much research needs to be done to confirm my findings, but there is always a beginning, and I have chosen to be that beginning.

You can call me Gage. I am a seven-year combat war veteran and a licensed advanced cardiac and trauma paramedic (19 years), and I was a fire fighter for five years in Dearborn. I served as a 1st Recon LAV FMF combat medic during the Kuwait Liberation War, I have been a Worldwide Personal Protective Securities (WPPS) high threat security specialist, and I have been a combat tactical shooter and TCCC (Tactical Combat Casualty Care) medic for the State Department and Department of Defense in Iraq and Afghanistan.

During this time, I have also been divorced twice and have a 12-year-old daughter, Sophia. Each time I went to war, I came back to people that had grown up or grown older. And I had to face them after long absences with a new problem: Multi-level Post Traumatic Stress Disorder. At least that is what the psychologists called it. This book is a story that will hit home for a lot of soldiers. It is one of bravery, stupidity, and luck that culminated in what I believe to be a cure for PTSD. There is hope out there, my friends. You no longer have to miss the wars you hate. Today there is only one battle that interests me—the battle to make cannabis a widely accepted *salvation* for PTSD.

CHAPTER 1

INTO THE FRAY

"Why is marijuana against the law?
It grows naturally upon our planet.
Doesn't the idea of making nature against
the law seem to you a bit . . . unnatural?"
BILL HICKS

They called it Sniper's Alley—a thin, winding road that snaked through the windy Sar-Hawza district with a wealth of blind spots and enough high ground to make it a favorite for Tali snipers. They would often let the enemy travel into the mountain, but once you came back down again, it was open season.

We received our orders for a routine scouting mission up in the Hindu Kush Mountains, hard along the Pakistan border directly through Sniper's Alley, that day. Over the past six months, my team had been sent out on several different scouting missions to recon various locations, collecting land surveys, images, and intelligence on the area.

We were paid High Threat Security Contractors who were tasked as a part of the Provincial Reconstruction and Security Buildup of Afghanistan, scouting for an RSSS project 8000 feet in the mountains, where the risk was high and the temperatures bitterly low, an expected zero degrees in all directions. It was a normal day for my team; we were handpicked for the job.

We would gear up, go out, do the recon, and return, hopefully with no casualties. It was a good day when no one was killed or injured. Our objective: to find a suitable spot to build the new Afghan Forwarding Operating Base.

A small Afghan National Police camp was already established, but all we had were GPS coordinates to get us there. Logistics were already arriving at basecamp, so we needed to move fast. Little did we know that our coordinates that day would be hampered by poor weather, sending us 1000 meters off course! Everything always looked the same out there—dry and desolate, like brown canvas stretched over rocks.

Our main role would be to collect as much information as we could while assessing the security threats in the area. That was all we knew and all we needed to know. It took three days to plan ahead for this mission and an evening's worth of running through our final plans before we were prepared to open the gate and leave the compound.

You were not safe from death inside our small basecamp, Camp KKG. We shared a common wall with a new Afghan Super FOB, where a battalion of soldiers were living and training. With only 400 friendlies at your back, you had to assume the moment you left the gates you were in someone's gun sights. My team, Task Force Dragon Slayer, always chose a different time to leave the gates. Routine was a death sentence in enemy territory.

We decided to leave that morning at 4:30, when it was still dark. It was a viciously cold November, and it had been snowing off and on at the time for over a month already. In the crisp moonlight above the compound, I could already see the towering Hindu Kush swathed in snow. Even the barren farmlands had a liberal dusting of it down in the valley.

There were times when I would stand on top of our MRAP and look out over the landscape in every direction. It was always breathtaking—the kind of majestic scenery you see in *National Geographic*, with peaks so high they poked holes through the clouds that drifted at an unimaginable altitude overhead.

This time, my team would be in a two-car package. The Dragon Slayer was one of the best teams in the compound. Made up of four men that day, we were one short on most occasions, and it was Danny Sanchez's turn to rotate out for some well-deserved R&R. So Mike White, Matt Deem, Jack Dixon, and I geared up for the mission.

Sniper's Alley was no joke. Mike was in the lead vehicle as VC (Vehicle Command) and team command, call sign: Archangel. He had lived in Georgia his whole life, swore like only a Georgian could, and was always good for a story or a drunken blitz. His beard suited his hard exterior, but all the guys who knew him best understood that of all of us, Mike had the biggest heart.

Matt was another Georgian white boy, with an extensive career in the military before joining the contracting niche. Like Mike and me, he was never at home, so many of his relationships failed, and like us, he loved to drink. Known for his reddish-brown beard and long hair, Matt had a great sense of humor rivaled only by Jack's.

Intimidating to look at but quiet by nature, Matt ate like a horse and did pull-ups like a national champion. Then there was Jack, call sign: Dir'tay from the movie *Joe Dirt*. The tallest of us, Jack loved sports and gymming most of all and was a big guy. He spoke with a Kentucky accent, and we would regularly tease him about being a redneck.

If we ever had a problem getting something from someone, Jack would step in as our PR guy. As a Marine sniper, he was also popular with the ladies and spent a lot of time online flirting with a plethora of them. Team Dragon Slayer was a formidable force, not just appearance-wise; we had a bond from running ops together.

That morning, the quiet outside was deafening. That is when movement becomes urgent and unsettling. We established radio communication with the base and then headed out. Jack drove the lead vehicle, with Mike riding shotgun on tactical command. Matt drove the second vehicle with me in the tactical command spot.

Today we would be driving white, armored land cruisers, two cars with the four of us in them. The moment the gate swung shut behind us, we were all in it. Things like rank and position rarely carried a whole lot of weight in the field. Respect had to be earned because your life was constantly at risk. It was you and the man on your right, and you were both accountable for your actions. It was Mike's job to get us back alive.

The trip took us to Camp Sharana first, where our HQ was. Jack hopped out of the car for a while to grab some energy drinks and get a take on what had been happening in the Sar Hawza District recently. After 15 minutes, we left the last bastion of safety behind.

Our mission took us down a lot of dirt roads, where occasionally we would pass a man on his donkey or a small motorcycle putting along at half speed.

It gave us time to engage in the normal bullshit. With fifty miles left to drive, we had more than enough opportunity to gauge the mental state of each team member. On any given day, this was always the most important thing. When a teammate's mind is not focused on the mission, it puts everyone at risk.

When you spend a lot of time in a warzone, you learn to leave your baggage back in the States. Alcoholism was a vocational hazard, and divorce was rampant—so there was always something going on that might impact the man next to you. It becomes second nature to probe, listen, and ask questions.

Out there, nothing matters but your integrity and whether or not you are paying attention to the situation at hand. A brief slip of focus can cost an entire team their lives. No one wanted their head blown off because the guy next to them was more focused on who might be shagging their girlfriend back at home than on situational awareness.

Mike was a great example of a war-ravaged soldier. He bore all the common marks of his trade: an enduring love for the bottle and two ex-wives back in America. Like me, he had a college degree tucked behind a beard and a baseball cap. Thanks to his years of overseas private contracting experience, Mike always had a story to tell.

To his credit, he was also smart enough to leave his drama at home. We had a small team, and there was enough drama brewing between us without the ongoing soap opera of our home lives causing additional stress. Mike's last divorce had been an apocalypse of sorts, but he never did let any of that impact his performance out on a mission.

It is not easy to perform for your men when life back at home has become the real war. I met Mike down in Kabul, and whether from fate or circumstance, we ran into each other again a couple weeks later at a FOB. I have been working with him ever since. Mike is a battle buddy, a brother for life; we have seen it all together.

Matt was a military man through and through, a kinder version of Mike really. With a pack of kids back home, he was all about supporting his family. He barely said a word until you put a beer in his hands, and then you could see he had a six-foot personality to match his height. The only person I had ever seen eat as much as Matt was Jack.

Perhaps it was his love of food that always weighed him down, although he was as lean as any of us. Matt would never rush for anything—gliding by slowly like he was on a beach somewhere, with all the time in the world. Jack, though, was a voracious eater, and he always managed to get some on himself. He quickly became known as the "food pig" of the group, but it suited his jovial nature.

As we drove along in our armored cars, the land leveled out, and suddenly a small village loomed ahead of us. Behind the village, the tall Hindu Kush rose high into the clouds, disappearing into a curtain of smoky morning mist. We followed our GPS coordinates so that we could get as close to our location as possible.

It was inevitable that at some point, we would have to walk some way. There was a small command post established beyond the village, with two guards who leered at us as we rolled by. They clung to their PKMs, trigger ready as they tracked our movement up the mountain. The terrain started getting bumpy and rough, and we knew it would not be long now.

Huge boulders and cavernous crevasses littered the mountainside, causing melting snow caps to run off the Kush Mountains and forming streams and inlets every now and then. Both drivers stopped, and we dismounted, preparing to walk the rest of the way. Jack stayed with the vehicles to watch over them and to maintain comms with our tactical operation command in Kabul and Sharana.

We breathed in that cold mountain air and pushed forward towards the huge mountain ahead, looking for a GPS location that was probably going to be shit in the first place. We found out later we were miles off target. Our three-man team trudged through the dirt and snow in full gear, for about five to six clicks. Eventually, we came upon a spot that had to be the location, or so we thought.

We sprang into gear and immediately began to map the coordinates, conducting a land survey and taking pictures. The guys liked to joke around a bit on the radios to ease the tension. Better to joke about Matt's bowlegs than to think about a Tali sniper having your head in their sights. When the job was done, we started to pack the gear.

Then something caught Mike's attention—a flash of something in the distance or movement that was foreign to the landscape. He walked towards the movement and after a few meters, came upon two large rock faces. Looking through his M-4 scope, he spotted two sheep gingerly moving over the mountain side. "Been doing this too long," he muttered. Deciding to take advantage of his distance from us, he unzipped his pants.

"Hey, Gage! There's something over here you might want to see," he called to me.

"Oh yeah? Finally found it yourself?" I joked, sidling over to him.

"Found something all right," said Mike, looking down off the rock face.

"Let me know if you need a stronger scope so that we can

all help Mike find it," called Matt as he continued to pack our gear away for transport.

"Fuck you and your beard, Matt," Mike called back smiling. "Just get over here, Doc." I arrived, wondering what could be so interesting about some random goats and sheep in the distance.

"Don't look there—look here," said Mike, guiding my scope. I walked around a large rock, and there, between two faces, was an opening about five feet wide from east to west. I could smell it before I could see it. A pungent odor washed over me, accosting my senses—but it did not register until I saw them. Three short, bushy green and purple cannabis plants stood protruding from the rock face below.

I stared transfixed by the resinous trichomes that were glistening off the round, purple buds as the morning sun rose like a flag hoisted over the snowy mountain caps. A smile spread across my face, and I bent down in front of the three plants, leaning into the fat, sticky bud at the very apex of the plant.

"Is someone growing these up here?" Mike asked me.

"It's possible. No one could just stumble on these unless they knew where to look...but then, maybe that's why they are still here. No one has found them yet," I said.

My mind raced enthusiastically, seeing the land in a new light. There were no tracks and no trails leading from the plants. I squeezed the top head between my fingers and took a lingering breath directly from the fragrant bud. Peculiar. We were in the second week of November, and outdoor was usually harvested in late October, maybe early November. The plants were in their prime, locked in time by the mountain freeze. With one to two inches of snow on the ground, these 10 plants should not be in such great condition.

"Damn, is this what I think it is?" I smelled the plant next to it.

Mike was staring at me curiously with a broad grin on his face. "Weren't you just talking about the medical miracle that exists in this plant?"

I nodded. "What is the difference between divine intervention and dumb luck?" I asked him in return. He shrugged.

"One's perfection and divine protection are directly proportional. That divine protection is great in some people, absent in others, and comes in varying degrees all according to each individual's perfection. The confusion comes in because each of us perceives miracles and divine intervention differently."

"What the fuck are you talking about, man?" he responded.

"Listen, bro, if all the shit that happens on earth is a miracle, then the next question needs to be—how do you distinguish which ones are meant for you and which are not?" I enthused.

"Dunno," Mike said, doing his perimeter check.

"Everything that happens to all of us here on earth is ultimately God's plan at work, but that doesn't mean it is God's will. Luck deals with the ongoing design of earthly occurrence and matter; intervention refers to something different—God's will." Truthfully, I had never been a religious person, but I did have faith in possibility. I knew Mike was a believer, so I thought it best to approach him on these terms.

"Unless you are a prophet, no one knows the difference between luck and divine intervention, because no one knows God's mind," Mike said directly, scanning the horizon.

"Agreed," I said. "The only way we poor bastards would ever know for certain is if God actually tells us."

Mike looked back at me a little irritated. "So what is God telling you, Doc?"

I rose on my haunches, reaching out for Mike's flak jacket, and pulled him down to my level. We both crouched before the plants while continuing our automatic assessment of our surroundings. "Remember what I was telling you about all the ways that this plant can help people? Imagine if you took that same medicine and then super powered it."

"So you would get super high?" he said, throwing me a cheeky look.

"Maybe, but that's not the point. You could create a stronger medicine from it for people that need it. This isn't just a plant, bro; it's a purple and green miracle. It shouldn't even be growing up here at this altitude! It looks like someone has been caring for them in this cold, but there are no traces of anyone ever being here."

"How do you know it's a miracle plant? Looks like normal bud to me," he responded, shifting his gear.

"You can see right here that the small stems at the bottom have been cut off so that the larger ones on top flower bigger and are healthier on harvest. They should have been harvested by now, actually," I said puzzled.

"It seems like the cold temperatures at night have kept them almost frozen all this time. I bet with all the action, the OGA and SF guys have been coming through here a lot. They might have scared this grower off. Who knows?"

"Well, we should just leave them right the fuck alone and roll outta here before this guy decides he wants his shit and brings a horde of his trigger happy Tali-buddies up here," Mike said nervously. "It could just be some local farmer who has been growing it for medicine or something. The locals know the restorative power these kush plants have. Why do you think it's the only thing growing up here right now?"

I stared intently into Mike's face. I could see that he was getting antsy. "This is no ordinary weed, bro, and we are bringing it back with us," I said, surprising myself.

"Hell no, Doc," proested Mike, "Coming back with us? No way."

I called on the radio and asked Jack to grab a couple trash bags from under the back seat and my Blackhawk Medic Bag directly behind the back seat of the LC and hand it off to Matt to bring up to me.

Matt called back asking, "Y'all okay?"

I called back and told Matt, "Yeah, we're good, bro...but I think Mike is still trying to find it." Matt just giggled in his low chuckle yet cheery tone.

As Matt was walking back with the black medic bag, I continued to inspect the plants. Mike asked me, "So what's up with the extra medic bag?" I then began wrenching the frozen plants from the ground with my Oakley tactical gloves on. I managed to remove a few plants without much damage.

"It doesn't feel right to just take it. We have to leave something of equal value," I responded as Matt was handing the medic bag to Mike, who then strongly dropped the bag right next to me. I then grabbed it and rested the medic bag securely between two rocks as I said to Matt "Thanks, bro."

Matt was just staring at the plants with his mouth half open but just kept quiet.

"You're crazy," said Mike as the three of us headed back to Jack.

"What the hell, Doc!" called Mike. "You're leaving a fully stocked medic bag here for someone that might be an RPG-carrying enemy?"

"It's my own personal fully stocked medic bag, and yes, I am."

"How much is this shit even worth undried, looking all dirty and smelling like hell?" Mike pressed.

"Well, Sally, in my professional opinion, we would not have enough money to cover this discovery even if we combined our salaries for the rest of our lives, if it turns out to be the strain that cures a major disease."

There we were at 8000 feet, freezing our asses off, and the one thing that I might have never thought possible was just handed over to me. Before we loaded the cars, Mike stopped me. "Are these plants really worth losing every fucking thing you have, including your life and ours?" he asked.

I responded in earnest, "I believe so."

"Can you guarantee that we will not get screwed when you get nailed for this?" he pushed.

"I can't."

A moment passed, and the decision was made. The drive back was twice as tense because of the new acquisition. Not only did we have to worry about enemy snipers, but now we had an illegal bag full of cannabis plants in our land cruiser. But it turned out the genetics in those seeds surpassed any other Afghan cannabis that had ever been documented in those extreme conditions. Truly divine providence.

CHAPTER 2

A NECESSARY RISK

"Don't criticize a snake for not having a horn;
for all you know it may someday become a dragon."

UNKNOWN

It turned out Matt and Jack were almost as excited about the cannabis plant discovery as I was. Being the team leader, Mike had reason to worry, although he went along with me all the same. Some risks in life are worth taking. It was a long and dangerous ride back to the base. The trip back was always more perilous than heading out.

It was not uncommon for enemy troops to allow you free passage up the mountain only to savagely attack you on your way down. Sniper's Alley was justly named, and many a soldier had met their end at the hand of a bullet from nowhere. The Taliban would love to transform a casual convoy of four guys into a batch of sitting ducks if they could.

The mountains rose around us, with too many nooks and crannies where Tali soldiers could hide in plain sight. It was always an unnerving ride, and all of our senses were extra heightened on the road back to Camp Ghazni. I glanced at Mike in the vehicle ahead; I could see he was uncomfortable about my decision to secure the plants.

He stared straight ahead, transfixed on the road. His rigid glower reminded me of my breach of protocol constantly, and even Matt had fallen silent since loading the plants in the car. No one was talking, and it was enough to make me doubt my actions. I got back to watch out for snipers. At the same time, my head was buzzing with the discovery of those plants.

Those buds twinkled at me in my memory, basking in a silver sunlight. In my mind's eye, I could still see them and all the potential that they held. In the cannabis community, the search for a new strain of landrace cannabis was the stuff of legend. People would travel all over the world in the hopes of discovering a rare find like this. Afghanistan was famous for producing the best indica in the world, a strain well known in the medical community.

Inside me, the excitement grew—even in that rigid silence. Who knew what medical benefits this particular plant might bring to the world? The potential was so high I could barely stifle a smile. I felt like primitive man after the discovery of fire, racing back to a frozen village with a glowing ember of hope.

But it was so much more than that. I had invested a lot of time and effort into cannabis research after the recent discoveries in the modern medical community. Locked in these unassuming cannabis plants were the gifts of healing and higher consciousness. I knew it was dangerous to throw caution to the winds, but it had to be done. Discoveries were made at awkward times in history, and you had to be bold to see them through.

Since I had returned from the Iraq War three years earlier, medical cannabis had become a personal research mission of mine. As someone who had always been desperate to help others, I happened on the miracles of cannabis for PTSD quite incidentally. *So what if it was my time*, I thought to myself. I could accept that. I could meet this challenge. Would you have done the same?

After too many days of swallowing mortar rounds in combat-ruined places like Basra and seeing grown men shredded through the grinder of tactical warfare, my PTSD reared when I returned home. Seeing grown men torn apart by bullets and bombs sets your brain on record. You capture snippets of these images, and they play in your mind on a loop.

The memory pulls you back into the moment, and soon your whole body is back in that place. Each time you close your eyes, it sets your life on fire as you become an unwilling casualty of the trauma. The trauma cycles through you like a sowing machine, stitching the worst memories of your time in combat together, a seamless collection of death that stabs at you with every thrust of the needle.

I got home that year, my mental state a smoldering heap of panic, survivor guilt, and memories that had been stitched onto the back of my eyelids. I needed help to function, and so I was put on many medications that my doctors said would help me. The medicine seemed to help in the beginning, but then it turned on me.

My infrequent IBS became a daily nuisance, which drained me of my energy. The pain medication they put me on had me feeling like a drug addict, strung out and too unmotivated on some days to do the most basic things. It became hard to live in a constant screen of lethargy, shielded from myself by a chemical mixture that swished around my brain, making me seasick on dry land.

The Cymbalta they had me on was even worse. Still prone to the follies of self-medication with alcohol, I mixed these two drugs indiscriminately and found out the hard way that this was a poor decision to have made.

One day during the move up north by myself, I lost self-control and ended up in jail for three nights and three days in complete isolation. I was being ripped apart from this on the inside, alone with all of my thoughts, believing I had just lost everything, including the seeds, and separated from everyone and everything I loved and valued in my life. I felt like a marionette without a puppeteer.

My life back home in the States no longer made sense. I had become a square peg that did not fit into my circular home life anymore. I started to lose all sense of myself, drifting in and out of awareness like my internal light was flickering and wanted to burst. I had to rush back to Afghanistan as a contractor to quiet the voices in my head.

At that stage, things had unraveled to the point where my only options were return to war or turn the light off forever. I ran back into the arms of combat. When I next returned home, a friend of mine turned me onto some good bud one day, just as the cannabis legalization movement was heating up.

Nothing could have prepared me for what happened. I smoked, and suddenly all was quiet. The mania receded, my depression vanished, and all of the bi-polar, suicidal madness came to a screeching halt. This might seem like nothing to you, but for me, it changed my life. For the first time in years, I was no longer at war.

It was like someone had replaced my internal light with an energy saver bulb! Like someone had stepped inside my head and done a bit of spring cleaning. The clutter had settled, and my spirit was calm once again. All at once, everything came back into sharp focus. The heightened state I had been forced to adopt as a soldier leveled out.

From that miraculous day on, I had a new mission. I needed to understand why cannabis could cure my PTSD in three seconds and yet it was never recommended to me. I had to know why it succeeded where all the other modern medicines had failed. I believe my first thought that day was, "Holy Jesus, all this grief for nothing."

I decided then and there to learn all I could about cannabis, its medical uses, and how to grow it to produce medical grade bud. The wife and I started to grow it in our basement—admittedly, the worst location possible to grow such a precious plant, but we still had to try and yet exercise caution at the same time.

I discovered that if I treated my PTSD with marijuana, it gave me the half second of extra time I needed to make the right decisions in my life instead of flying off the handle. Logic became clear, my focus was tightened, and empathy became more valued. The cost of this was incalculable for me. I became a fierce advocate for the use of medical cannabis, especially for mental disorders or what I call mental distractions. (I believe that PTSD is not a mental disorder; it is a mental illness or what I like to call mental distractions. It just depends on how many distractions there are, how deep they scar, and how well you deal with it at the time.)

I immersed myself in all the education I could find, including Jorge Cervantes book, *The Marijuana Bible*, and soon my knowledge on medical marijuana exploded. Today medical marijuana is legal in 23 states, and nine more are poised to legalize it. In fact, right now, Michigan is on the 2016 ballot for marijuana legalization. America has come a long way in a short time thanks to the pioneers that started and supported cannabis legalization, but we still have a much longer road to travel.

The rampant demonization of this innocent, healing plant has done its damage over the past 70 years. Luckily, international research that has gone on since the '60s has plugged a lot of holes. Doctors in Israel were the first to isolate THC and CBD for medical treatments. They regularly use cannabis to treat cancer, epilepsy, Parkinson's disease, and mental disorders.

Plants with a higher CBD[1] content are said to pack the most punch for people with PTSD and other anxiety-related disorders. On the list of incredible cures, cannabis has successfully treated mood disorders, Tourette's syndrome, obsessive compulsive disorder, cancer, neurological disorders, multiple sclerosis, seizure disorders, autism, obesity, arthritis, heart disease, insomnia, and pain—just for starters.

When my experience with cannabis had sunk in a little deeper, I developed an appreciation for my mother's cannabis use. The entire time she had been self-medicating her own PTSD, finding that it helped but never truly able to free herself from society's "drug" stigma. In the space of 30 seconds, I became ashamed that I had scolded her for using it. Somewhere in her heart she already knew what I was only just discovering. Cannabis turns the volume down on the chaos.

---

1   Jen Christensen, 10 Diseases Where Medical Marijuana Could Have Impact, http://edition.cnn.com/2015/04/15/ health/marijuana-medical-advances/

It was a hard lesson to learn. My mother is gone now. She will never know that her instincts were right. I often wonder if cannabis had been a medicine back then, if she would have lived longer and been happier. It will always be my darkest regret and a key motivation in my future dealings with this miracle plant.

The more I studied, the more it blew my mind that cannabis was such an effective PTSD cure, yet so many soldiers were struggling with medications that made them worse off than before. As a paramedic, I regularly came across people who had medicine bags full of the junk that was supposed to be helping them.

I realized there was a lot more to weed than anyone really understood. There were different strains, as varied as different off the shelf medications—some could trigger panic, while others would heal it! It depended mostly on the THC–CBD balance, which are synergistic to each other; when one goes up, the other goes down. This explained why common street weed would sometimes cause people problems.

Over several decades, it was bred for a high THC content, the psychoactive property in weed, instead of a high CBD content, which helps promote internal healing. My passion for medical cannabis research grew, along with several plants I was tending to in my basement. I went from a man who was imploding to a man with a mission.

In my humble opinion, medical cannabis has the potential to save thousands of soldiers' lives. It can help to heal their PTSD symptoms, and it will not shorten their lifespans or cause disease to start up in other places in the body. In almost every way, this little plant became the answer to a question I had been asking since first returning from war. When will the chaos stop?

"Right now," said that cannabis treatment. It was around this time I became aware of a myth that was deeply entrenched in the cannabis community. I learned that somewhere in the world, no one knew where, but quite possibly high up in the Hindu Kush, was a primeval strain of bud.

It is a strain so powerful that it can cure diseases more effectively than anything the world has ever seen. This story is told often among cannabis entrepreneurs, who explore remote parts of the world searching for new natural strains for medicinal benefits. And there, in the back seat of my land cruiser, was possibly the Holy Grail.

I might have the oldest, most potent natural cannabis strain known to man stashed away in a black garbage bag behind me. You cannot blame me for calling it divine providence. The chances that we would be up there, in the middle of nowhere in the Hindu Kush, and to have stumbled upon such a rare find in winter was nothing short of a miracle.

There was simply no way that Mike or any of the other guys would have been able to stop me. I had spoken with them about it many times before that, and they knew how I felt about it. I believe they went along with it because they realized how important it was to me. This miracle needed to be released into the world, and I had the only known strain. The radio crackled, dragging me out of my reverie.

It was the Special Forces team checking in with an update. An enemy target up ahead had been neutralized, so we should have no trouble getting back to base. As we arrived back at camp unmolested by enemy troops, Mike jumped out of the vehicle ahead of Matt and me and made a beeline for me.

"Your fucking vehicle stinks; at least go clean it out," he said, peering suspiciously at the black bag of offending plants. Matt and I drove to the back of the compound and did as we were told. In the meantime, Mike and Jack briefed HQ on our successful mission.

Once we had aired out the vehicle, I smuggled the bags over to my hooch and spread the plants out on the floor. I marveled at them, but it was tinged with guilt. I knew at any time I could be discovered and my entire team would lose their jobs, clearances, and futures. The deed had been done, but it was a deed that came steeped in risk.

I started off by documenting the discovery. I placed a Coke can among the plants for scale and took some pictures. There were two females, and the rest of the plants were males. Seeds fell out of the plant as they skated across the floor, so I collected them in a container. I bagged each plant separately, slipped around to the back of my hooch, and hid them.

I needed to get those genetics back to the States, but how? All that night I lay in my bed thinking hard about my options. I knew one thing—this strain needed to be tested, and I was the guy who was going to do it. When I eventually left for home with the seeds a few months down the track, an hour later, an Afghan soldier opened fire on an Army officer while he was in the super FOB next door. Mike, Matt, and Jack were the first on the scene. They described it to me as a "slaughter." What was reported and what really happened no one will ever know. But Mike insisted that I was one lucky son of a bitch for getting out of there the hour before this happened with my life and with the seeds in hand.

A few days after I found the strain, we were given another mission. It was the same as the previous one: gear up, get in, get out, and do not get killed in the process. The barren Afghan countryside always bothered me. Except for the mountain scenes or the occasional irrigated valley, the dry, reddish terrain was monotonous and unchanging.

The mud brick villages all looked alike: sad, crumbling hovels as bad as any Third World slum I had ever seen. We passed through yet another featureless village with villagers walking along the road. Mothers held their daughters' hands, and boys walked alongside their fathers, herding goats to an undisclosed location.

I would often watch these families and think of home. Despite being in a war-torn country, they were a unit: a mother and father and the kids—something I had never known. Distant memories of another life came back to me, as they often did on long stretches of identical road. The most burning…my absent father.

My last normal memory of the man was when we were building a large model motorcycle together down in our basement. In truth, I do not remember much from my early childhood. Memories would come in snatches, triggered by external events that were out of my control. Today they were coming in rapid flashes.

Born in St. Louis, my family moved to Colorado. It was me, my mother and father, and my little sister Michelle. When I was eight years old, my father disappeared for three whole days. I remember my mother was frantic. She called the police, the local hospitals, and the morgue but to no avail. She put us in the car, and we spent the night searching for him.

Suddenly, the next day, my father reappeared again. My mother took him into the back room, and a fight broke out. I heard shouting and tears and my father's voice. When I was older, I learned that he had been seeing another woman and had begged forgiveness from my mom that day. Once again, we would move to get a fresh start somewhere new.

The following weeks were strained. I watched as all the

furnishings in our house were sold. All we had left was a meager handful of personal belongings. The next day after school, we busied ourselves packing the final remains of the house. But my father never came home from work that day.

Again, my sister and I spent the night in my mom's car, driving around in search of my father. The two of us woke the next morning in a parking lot to the sound of my mother crying. "There's nothing left," she said, "and this time he's not coming back." From that moment, I knew that I would have to take care of my mom so that she could care for us.

My father had taken the proceeds from the house and had run off with his girlfriend. Once the dust had settled, my mother got in touch with her parents, and they sent us enough money to make the trip to Dearborn Heights, Michigan. What little we still owned could fit into our car. We filled the car with gas and headed east.

My grandfather built one of the first homes in the city along Gully road. We lived there for a few months, but it never really felt like home to me. I spent a lot of my time wondering whether or not I could sit on any of their plastic-covered furniture. It was all too stiff and formal for my liking. So my mother arranged an apartment for us in Taylor.

She was a high school graduate and had a couple of shots of herself posing for a car magazine that she added to her resume. The job search began. Luckily, my mother had always been great with people. She became good friends with the manager of our apartment complex, and she helped my mom get her complex manager's license. This was a great opportunity for my mom because it guaranteed a roof over our heads and enough money to put food on the table. Shortly afterwards, she landed a job managing an apartment complex just down the block from where we lived. We moved and found a measure of stability there.

Then she met Sid, a heavy drinker who was also in complex management. The two of them would go out and party all night together. I had to make dinner for my sister and me and took over a lot of responsibilities from my mother. In the mornings, I made breakfast and got Michelle ready for school, and when I got back from class, there would be a note on the fridge: "Make dinner."

At the age of 10, I was already an expert in whipping up a roast beef dinner with gravy, mashed potatoes, canned corn, and biscuits. But I was not Micki's mother or father—this is the nickname I had for her. She complained constantly about missing my father. My mother was always working, and she sacrificed a lot for us kids.

She had subtle ways of letting me know about the people in the complex so that I was informed. Even though she was a genuinely good person, my mother had serious abandonment issues of her own. One night Sid became sick of hearing my sister complain about missing her dad.

"If she wants to go, just fucking send her. Christ, I'll pay her fare myself; it's one less mouth to feed!" My sister degenerated into spasms of grief, which Sid seemed to enjoy. My mother, however, would support him and not my sister. She always seemed a little more irritated with Micki than she should have been.

Somehow my mother located my father and sent Micki off to live with him. I wondered why I could not go live with him too, but I thought it best not to ask. We were poor, living from paycheck to paycheck, and my mother never did recover from what my dad did to her. Sid was a constant problem, a total bastard.

He made me feel unwelcome in my own house, and when he spoke to me, I could feel the disdain dripping off his chin. My mother focused on Sid and forgot me. Looking back, I know she was only trying to cope, but it was hard nonetheless. They decided to look for a complex to manage together as a couple.

For those few weeks they were away training in Ohio, I stayed with my friend Jose. We would revel in the hip-hop scene and stayed up all night listening to music. In the end, I had to leave, and we moved to Ohio. If you lived in an apartment there, you were considered trash. Plus, Sid was taking more and more advantage of my mother, who was doing all the work. She put in 18 hour days while Sid sat around drinking all day.

One night the two of them came home drunk. My mother had fallen to the ground, so I rushed outside to help. Still half asleep, I posed a question at Sid, who promptly attacked me. "Is it late?" I said. He took it badly and punched me in the gut then wrapped his arms around my neck. I could not breathe, and everything went dark.

The next day I had a lot of bruises to hide, but that night was never spoken about again. Micki wanted to come home, which was causing constant screaming matches in the apartment between my mother and Sid. I boiled internally from the hatred that I nurtured for that guy. I would dream about cutting his throat as he slept.

One night, Sid went out and my mother came storming into my room, waking me from a dead sleep. She had been crying and was mildly hysterical. "We're leaving" she said, and we did. I had a few minutes to pack some things into a bag, and the two of us took off down the road together. I left a lot of things behind, but it was worth it to never see Sid again.

Unfortunately, my mom had the worst taste in men. There were seven dads, all carbon copies of Sid who slid in and out of our lives over the years. Because of this, we moved from place to place, never settling in a real home and never really having any stability. I was enrolled in so many schools I never had any real friends.

It was not for lack of trying, I was always well liked but little known. I would make friends fast but would soon lose contact with them after we moved. No one ever kept in contact with me. Time, it seems, is what true friendships are made of. The military always felt more like my real home, perhaps because it was constantly moving and people changed all the time.

Looking back, my childhood perfectly positioned me for a career in the military. I was a team player, great with people thanks to my mom, and tough enough to handle high stress situations thanks to the people she dated. All I needed was training, but first I would have to hit rock bottom as a teenager.

CHAPTER 3

SHOTS FIRED

"Marijuana is one of the safest,
therapeutically active substances known to man."
JUDGE FRANCIS YOUNG (DEA)

The land cruisers trundled by as we headed towards our new mission location. Mike had been at me because of the plants, and I could not blame him for that. I was playing a dangerous game with all of their careers.

"Are you done fantasizing now?" he would say to me. "Can we get rid of those fucking plants before we all end up fired? You are never going to find a safe way to get those things back into the States. Just face it, Doc."

It was sage advice, to be sure. But I could not bring myself to throw away the possibilities that lay in those black plastic bags behind my hooch back at the FOB. Like a couple of dead bodies, they were becoming a bigger distraction than they were worth.

Then, the shit hit the fan—the kind that had nothing to do with some harmless plants that were innocently stowed away at basecamp.

While we began walking towards a construction site where a new ANP (Afghan National Police) station was to be constructed, we chose a day when there were no workers on sight, but we were ambushed. We had stopped for a moment to inspect our immediate area and let Matt catch up a bit since his stagger was a bit slower than ours. Mike started to tell one of his "No shit, there I was" stories as I began to take note of the higher ground around us.

It was rocky and remote there, much like most of the landscape in Afghanistan. You are lucky if you get to hear the telltale signs of an ambush before anyone gets hurt. A loud, resonant crack or two pings off rocks close to your head, and you have seconds to react to save your own life.

As we all leapt for cover, the bullet melody continued playing off the nearby rock face. Mike dove behind a towering boulder, and I jumped into a deep crevasse. I did not see where Matt ended up. Each of us called out to make sure the others were not hit. Then Mike spoke, "What the fuck! Where the hell are the rounds coming from?"

Matt called out from under the LC, where he threw himself into what seemed to be home plate. "Up top, about 3 o'clock!" he shouted as the gravel spit from his beard.

Mike yelled back, "Anyone got a bead on these guys?"

"It's probably the fuckers who donated the weed," I joked.

"Real damn funny, Gage," Mike said, directing his attention to our vehicle. Jack was still inside it, head ducked down, just peering over the dash; he was the safest of all of us. "Jack, are there two shooters or just two shots?" was called into his handheld radio mic, which was located tightly attached to his KIT.

A strained voice came from inside the land cruiser. "I don't know, man. I heard two shots, but I don't see anything. What do you want me to do?"

"Stay in the vehicle and call this in," instructed Mike.

Nothing like a brush with death to remind everyone where we were. Jack got on the radio from his position in the vehicle and reported the shooting, using a selection of carefully constructed curse words.

"Gage, can you make it over to me?" called Mike. I peeked over the edge of my crevasse, and two more shots cracked off rocks on either side of me.

They had us pinned down.

I ducked back down, glad to still have my head. I did not know where the shots had come from or how close they had hit. All I knew was that I was in their sights. I was at the receiving end of a sniper's scope. Mike had the stronger position, so I had to make a run for it. If I stayed, I may only have had minutes before the shooter found a better angle.

I jumped out of my hole and made the mad dash for Mike's position. All around me bullets sang their deathly song, kicking up tufts of dirt and spraying me with debris. I nearly ran straight past Mike, but he was able to grab hold of my flak jacket and pulled me behind the boulder. "Fuck it," came Matt's voice as he scooted out from under the vehicle and ran bowlegged for our spot in a similar hail of bullets.

"Where's that God damn QRF (Quick Reaction Force)?" called Mike as Matt collapsed beside us, heaving.

"It's en route, but it may take up to half an hour," came Jack's disembodied voice.

"Excellent, we'll probably be dead by then," Mike responded, peering from behind the boulder. "Well, what do you want me to do?"

We were pinned in an area where Jack just could not get the LC to and far enough away to give any sniper a good shot.

"Relocate to wherever you feel safe, and ride it out. If it gets too hot on your end, make your way outta sight towards the direction the QRF are coming from, and don't let anymore holes get in my vic."

"Roger that."

As the land cruiser started up and roared some distance away, we dug ourselves in for the long wait. Our position was not the best, but it would give a superb shot a hard time. We had to trust in that. Sometimes that is all you can do to remain calm—trust.

The usual bickering and joking started up between the three of us, a natural survival reflex to defuse the tension. When I heard the word "'divorce," my mind hurtled back to my childhood. More a trial by fire than anything, my mother and I were never very far from total ruin. After leaving Sid, we arrived at my uncle's house in Akron, Ohio, to start over again.

After a time, my mother landed a job managing a huge apartment complex of her own. All of the tenants loved her. They would stop by to leave donations for us or just to say hello. My mother had a habit of sticking her neck out for the less fortunate, and she always made sure I knew which tenants were good and which were not.

I remember this one time she let a man she found sleeping outdoors at the complex stay with us for a short time. There was a small area in the basement that she fixed up nicely with a mattress on the floor with blankets and a pillow, a small chair, and some books. While I never quite understood that, I knew she had her reasons. It came from a good place. That was my mom—reckless, with a huge heart. She would regularly go without so that my sister and I had what we needed.

Back when Micki still lived with us, she even managed to come up with Christmas presents, although we were worse than broke. After my father and Sid, the general mood in the house was dark. I could not blame her; she had been through a lot and abandoned a lot. I can still feel that desperate desire I used to have to help her. I would often catch her in moments of despair and long to heal her broken heart.

Then, almost suddenly, she was okay again. She began dating and having fun, and the mood transformed from dark to positively enlivened. Not long after that, a man moved into our apartment. Yet again I was asked to call a stranger dad—a stranger who appeared to be no different than my father or Sid had when we had lived with them.

She never saw the resemblance. Thankfully, these relationships came and went. Like a long string of broken beads threaded throughout my life, they stepped in and out at different times. I gave up counting her list of "world's most awful men" when she hit seven. During this turbulent time, I did not go to the same school for any longer than two years straight.

We floated from town to town, complex to complex, until people were just blurred faces and random names. I learned how to make friends in an instant and to not get too attached to them either. I would give kids my stuff to make them like me and would go out of my way to connect with them. I developed a real talent for being the nicest guy on the block.

Because this never really made any difference, I also

became a loner and an outdoors kid. I was always covered in dirt from exploring the great outdoors. It did not matter how long it took or how bad it turned out; I made myself happy by creating things. It taught me to embrace creativity and become a fiercely independent human being.

For some people, independence is a natural process, but I did not really have any other choice. It was thrust upon me, so I did my best with it. In any event, it got me away from the mind-numbing effects of video games and television.

Then, in the early '80s, we moved out to sunny California, and my mom took a job managing an apartment complex on Hollywood Boulevard six blocks down from the Chinese Theatre. Micki had come back to live with us, but she soon fell in with a bad crowd that used to roam the strip. One day she came back home looking like Kiss in a skirt with an attitude to match. By then she pretty much ran away from home. We never had a solid relationship after that, Micki and I, and we never seemed to care enough to make one.

Those early days of my life taught me how to block things out, even my own family. I had started my freshman year in high school and got my ass kicked on campus three days in a row. I decided I had enjoyed enough of that, so I skipped school and went to the beach. There I discovered a passion for surfing. I already knew the ropes, but this was where I toned my wave skills.

Soon, every morning after saying goodbye to my mom and riding my bike out of sight, I would make a quick detour to anywhere between Marina Del Rey down to Palos Verdes to hit the waves, although Redondo was a favorite spot back then before the pier was destroyed by bad weather and turned into a horseshoe pier. I used my $5 lunch money to grab a Carne Asada burrito beans and rice from Roberto's after the morning surf. Sometimes I would stay at the beach all day, especially if times were rough. There was something about the rolling waves, the fresh sea-salt air, and the abundant animal life all around me that drew me there and calmed me. I would explore the city on the way home and was always careful to show up at home at the right time, like it was the end of my school day.

It was easy to fake a conversation about class with my mother. Each day was a new opportunity to survive, and I could not think beyond that. My mom had her endless boyfriend drama, my sister was a street kid, and school had become my personal torture chamber. If only those days on the beach had lasted! Three months in, my mother got a phone call from the high school principal.

"Aren't you supposed to have a son attending Hawthorne High?" asked the bored voice on the other end of the line.

"Of course," my mother replied. "Five days a week."

"Not for the last 13 weeks he hasn't!"

She busted me later that day. I did not see any point in lying, so I came clean. I told her I gave it my best, but once I started to fear for my life, I had to make a change, and I was not about to mess up our stability. It was just that when two days turned into ten, then into weeks, I just kept going with it because everything seemed to be going okay. "You'll have to make up for it over the summer," she told me. And that was that.

At this point, my mother had invited another son of a bitch into my life named Don. Much like Sid, Don had a wonderful way with alcohol. I learned very quickly to reserve my opinions when I was around him; he was not a fair or logical man. Muttering something under my breath might as well have been threatening him with a pistol. His fuse was short and always smoldering.

When Don got home that day, he was already drunk. But now he was pissed for another reason. I would have to stay home every day until summer school, and he did not like it. It would certainly interfere with his rigorous drinking schedule during the day. I soon realized that he was never sober.

Don was an asshole to me before he drank and a bigger one once he was drunk. A smack on the back of my head was his idea of a love tap. A surprise punch in the gut was his affectionate way of toughening me up. I was constantly on edge, but I never saw them coming. The man loved to catch me off guard, and he was good at it.

A day came when Don was stumbling around more than usual. I expected him to face plant into the carpet at any moment. I looked at him quizzically and asked if he thought he drank too much. He gazed back at me, his eyes unfocused and confused. His response was to take me down to his workshop in the apartment complex basement.

Don's official title was the maintenance guy for our block. There, he had his own private, fully-stocked fridge. "I'll tell you why I drink so much," he sank at me when we arrived. "Because if I didn't, you and your mother would drive me fucking crazy! Can I get this, can I get that? Always some God damned thing the two of you need. It pisses me off!"

He stood there, glassy-eyed and pathetic, too drunk to move or think with any kind of accuracy. I hoped his stupid diatribe would end soon. I did not know much, but I knew his despicable behavior had nothing to do with my mother or me. "I'll tell you what, you little shit. Let me show you what 'drinking too much' looks like. Let's have a shotgun beer contest." He opened the fridge, and the soft, glowing light inside revealed a multitude of liquors and beer. "Impressive, huh?"

I had never consumed alcohol before. From my past experience with my mother's boyfriends, all it did was make people stupid and fall down.

"What do you say?" he said, looking menacingly at me.

I agreed. I figured that by the time I finished my first can, Don would be passed out on the floor. It may have been my first time, but I was confident I could take him. I downed the first beer I ever drank in one gulp. I almost threw up. Don downed his like Kool Aid. It was my turn again, and I downed the second beer. Don stopped drinking and egged me on.

I had shot-gunned five beers before I threw it all up again, along with my morning breakfast. Don laughed his drunken ass off, until he started to dry heave. The two of us fled back upstairs to the apartment. Once we had arrived, Don was upset. His playful slaps turned into real punches. He did not need a reason; he was drunk. This time, though, so was I. With my mind swimming in beer and my inhibitions at an all-time low, I decided to hit back before my brain could formulate the thoughts. Don did not like that. He decided to teach me a lesson. After a dozen punches, one connecting with my nose and breaking it, I passed out on the floor in a pool of my own blood.

I do not remember why, but the moment I came around, I cleaned myself up and pretended nothing had ever happened. Funny the things you do when you are a child living in an adult's fucked up life.

Once I had finished summer school, my mother decided to take a new managing job close to San Diego. At the time, I had one of my first girlfriends, a tall blonde girl called Jeanie. Because of her, I did not want to move, knowing full well that I would never see her again. One evening when I was at Jeanie's house, something happened.

My mother had obviously wondered where I was, and Don had said that he would go looking for me. I know this because of what happened that night. Don has stopped off at the corner bar first. Then he took a slow cruise to Jeanie's house from the bar, which was three blocks west of where we stayed.

Jeanie and I were making out on the couch when the pounding came from the front door. "I know you're in there, you little fucker! Get your ass out here right now; your mother wants you home!" It was Don's drunken tones, the kind that usually came before the punching. I knew that I only had a second to react, to call his attention away from Jeanie and her house.

At any moment, he could barge in and would start beating on me. That could not happen. I told Jeanie to tell him that I had gone to the store and would be back soon. While she was telling him this through the door, I snuck out the second story back patio and ran around as if coming back from the store.

As I came walking up the sidewalk, Don wheeled around on the staircase, fuming. "What the fuck!" he shouted at me.

"What?" I shouted back, "I just returned some bottles for a refund at the store and was about to head home." I climbed into Don's car without being asked. He had parked it halfway onto the lawn, like only a total drunkard would.

He stared at me for a long time before starting the engine. The entire ride home, it was one monologue about how worried my mother was. According to Don, he had been looking for me all night. Back at the apartment, Don started up the stairs ahead of me, and I followed. When I heard my name, I looked up in time to catch a cowboy boot in the face.

Thrown back by the force of the drop kick, I tumbled down

the stairs and landed at the bottom, an assortment of twisted legs and arms. Don slowly made his way back down to me.

"What the fuck!" I screamed in pain. But Don was not finished. As I lay there on the floor, he began yelling and kicking at me until he ran out of steam. I do not know how long it took. All I remember is him warning me not to say anything to my mother about it. "You were in a fight, and I found you looking like this, didn't I?" he spat at me. "Say any different and I'll kill you."

I never did tell my mother the truth about what had happened. For the next year or so, this horrible secret bloomed between Don and me. I became his personal punching bag, and there was not a thing I could do about it. "What's the matter, punk?" he would yell at me, "Don't you have enough balls to fight back?"

On the few occasions when I did try to fight back, the beatings were predictably worse. He did not want me to fight back; he wanted an excuse to hit me harder. From the time he booted me down the stairs, I had a 95% blockage in the right side of my nose. It messed me up for a long time and made it hard for me to play sports or do rigorous activity.

Living with Don and his secret violence caused me to develop sleep apnea and sleeping disorders. There was never a moment around him when I was not walking on eggshells or dreaming about guns. Then one beautiful, sunny day, the owner of the apartments arrived to inspect the apartment complex.

Don was his usual charming, drunken self. They got into a heated argument, and Don was fired on the spot. That night, Don and my mother got into a nasty argument. Don was in a particularly violent mood because of his recent blunder into unemployment and, it was not long before words became slaps and slaps became punches.

When my mother tried to flee the apartment with my sister and me, Don punched her in the side of the head. I was suspended in slow motion, watching it happen. Unlike her, I knew what was coming, but Don was in such a rage I could not stop it. I did the best I could to catch her as she went limp from the blow, knocked out cold.

Enraged by the attack on my mother, I pounced on Don, swearing and swinging. The two of us went at it for some time. Blow for blow, I matched him. I had never fought as hard as that before, until I fell backwards, smashing into a large terracotta pot, gashing my thigh open. Blood spurted out all over me. The aloe vera plant was in ruins.

"Keep your blood to yourself, motherfucker," said Don, and he left. We never saw him again. I noticed a few days later that his stuff was gone from the apartment, but that was it.

I do not have many good memories of my mother, but one thing I do remember is that she loved music, especially rock-n-roll, and her favorite was always Bob Seger. I always knew she was in a good mood when Bob was on, and no matter what my thoughts were at the time, I was always happy to see her smile, especially when playing some Seger. One thing I remember is that she told me she used to put me in a bungee-cord bouncy contraption that hung in a doorway, and when she played music, I would bounce right on the beat every time, and this is when she knew I also had an ear for music.

Not long afterwards, we moved again—this time to Fallbrook in Northern San Diego County. The back gate of the Marine base Camp Pendleton became my back yard.

October arrived, and school had already been in full swing when I showed up to yet another class of strangers. I was a pro at blending in. I made some friends and joined the football and wrestling teams. I never had any parents show up to my tournaments, but I was careful to never miss any myself. Here, I felt like a real teenager for the first time.

I discovered why I hated beer during those months and did a lot of harmless stupid shit that teens do. I also fell in love with a beautiful redhead, Trisha, who became the center of my world. She seemed to heal the pain that I had lived with until then. With legs a mile long and the cutest freckles a person can have, it was my first real experience with love.

Schwarzenegger was an icon for a lot of boys my age, so I joined the Fallbrook Athletic Club and got into bodybuilding. One of my older gym buddies, Galen, who taught me how to play racquetball there from back then, went on to become an American Gladiator! Now he is an incredible trainer and volleyball coach. School clicked along as it does, but I rarely slept at home. It did not matter where I slept as long as there was a place for me to rest my head.

My mother remained single for a very long time after Don. She concentrated on managing her apartments and was happy for the most part. Then she began to mess around with an old friend of my father's. He lived in Michigan and would fly out to visit for a week at a time. The next thing I knew my mother decided she was moving us to Michigan, which was also her birthplace.

The two of them had worked out how to manage some apartments there together. Anything for her happiness, right? I was halfway through my senior year, in love for the first time, and happier than I had ever been in my entire life. I was not going anywhere. When I tried to tell her, we ended up in a giant screaming match.

Legally, I was too young to be out on my own, but I was too old for my mother to try to physically stop me from leaving. The mother of one of my best friends, Todd Rodriguez, came around to talk to my mother on hearing the news. She was single and sympathetic, so she told my mom that she would help a bit with rent, food, and utilities—at least until school ended.

My mother agreed against her will and left for Michigan to seek out her happy ending. I found a spot in my friend's garage with a twin bed and some hanging sheets for privacy and warmth. His mom managed to get a heating duct all set up for me so that I would not freeze through the winter and could finish my last semester of high school.

CHAPTER 4

MEDICAL MUSINGS

"The illegality of cannabis is outrageous, an impediment to full utilization of a drug which helps produce the serenity and insight, sensitivity and fellowship so desperately needed in this increasingly mad and dangerous world."

CARL SAGAN

My mother stepped on a plane and jetted off to her true love far away, leaving me behind in California to deal with my final school days alone. A few months later, my friend's mother got engaged. Great for her, not so good for me. Things quickly began to unravel once her new beau had moved in.

I was 17 when a few major consequences reared up like a frightened animal and kicked me in the jaw. First, I lost my job at the local factory where I worked to support myself. The old boss had sauntered onto the factory floor one day and fired me, along with 50 Mexican workers. "Downsizing"

I think he called it; the part we had been making for Robert Shaw Industries was discontinued.

I was downsized out of a livelihood, and with almost no support from my mom in Michigan, the real world came rushing up to greet me pretty fast. The new fiancé and I did not hit it off, and the climate in the house changed. When I had reached the fourth month of unemployment and was still unable to pay the arrears rent for my garage apartment, he made sure that I was kicked out. Trisha ended up with some military guy from the base, a Navy medic also I believe. He turned out to be a big cocaine addict and a bigger problem for Trish; bummer it turned out that way.

Goodbye, roof over my head. I found myself without a job, without any means to earn money, and without a place to sleep. Even worse, I did not know where my next meal was going to come from. I was destitute at 17. Luckily, I knew some questionable characters that knew how to navigate the rougher side of frugal living in sunny Cali.

They lived around Oceanside and were deeply involved in the new "crack" scene that was becoming such a hit in the neighborhood.

There I was, staying up all night with crack undesirables just to stay off the streets. I was smart enough to stay away from the drugs myself; they scared the shit out of me. I saw what they did to people, and I wanted a future.

I hated living with them, but the nights were getting colder, and sleeping in my car was uncomfortable and freezing. I did not even own a blanket. All I had to keep me warm were the clothes on my back, a habit I had picked up from my turbulent childhood. To this day, it is quite easy for me to just walk out the door with what I have on to tackle the next opportunity. One chilly California afternoon, one of my crack house friends asked me a favor.

He wanted a ride up to Orange County, where he had some kind of drug deal in the pipes. I was reluctant to get involved, but he offered me gas money, and I felt like I owed them a debt for helping me out, so off we went. The two of us stopped off at a mall in Orange County, where his transaction would take place.

I decided to go for a stroll through the shops. The plan was to meet him back at the car in 30 minutes—easy enough. After my mall tour, I was returning to the car when I noticed a large, vulnerable pyramid of comforters stacked up next to the door of a Bed, Bath & Beyond. I confess, the allure of a warm blanket was too much for me to ignore.

I snatched one in a hurry and made a beeline for the mall entrance. Just shy of my car, a mall cop cut me off and read me the riot act. "Hands up!" It was over. They ended up towing my car and carted me off to the Orange County jail. There, I got to enjoy my own bright orange jumpsuit for three solid days and nights while I was in lockup. I did not like how it felt.

I was dragged in front of a judge and slapped with a misdemeanor. The three days acted as my time served. I felt lucky to escape with my freedom after such an impulsive act, but once again, I had backed myself into a corner. My car was impounded, and I had no money to get it out. Now I had no job, no money, no home, and no car. Things were getting dire.

I spent two days on the streets, slowly making my way back to Oceanside. I was suspended in someone else's bleak reality; it did not feel real. With all of those cold hours of reflection, I settled on the only truth that mattered, the one that gave me hope. I knew I was a smart guy. I knew that there had to be more for me than this messed up situation suggested.

By the third day, I was trawling the streets of Carlsbad looking for my next meal. I found myself at another mall and headed straight for the food court. Often businesses would leave out food samples, so if you were clever about it, a few sweeps around the circuit and you could put together a decent meal for yourself. I would do it as many times as I could, until I was stuffed.

My belly full of tasty samples, I cruised around the mall feeling much happier than when I had entered. When I next raised my head, I happened to be standing outside of a recruitment office. I had never considered a life in the military before and had no intention of ever having one.

A young man strode out of the office towards me, and my heart fluttered. Good thing he kept walking; I thought he was trying to hand me a wad of brochures. If he had done that, I probably would have just cast them aside without a second thought. Phew! Dodged that bullet.

Speaking of bullets, back in the present, a couple more pinged off the large boulders that were sheltering Mike, Matt, and me from death. I glanced over to them and realized that we had been in an uncomfortable silence for too long. Those long silences can make a brave man tremble.

Mike had his head cocked back and was staring into the afternoon sky with his eyes shut. Sunlight, warmth—he was using it to ward off the panic. Matt had his head down on his knees, looking considerably concerned. The three of us were still sitting there, huddled behind those damn rocks waiting for the Quick Reaction Force to show up.

It had been more than 30 minutes, over an hour to be exact. An hour pinned in the wilderness can seem like an eternity. You can relive each day of your life in those eternal moments, until every tiny mistake you have ever made can seem like a death sentence that led you to your current predicament. You have to rage against panic like that.

I started ripping on the two of them again to ease the tension and poked holes in the clammy silence. I went through the motions, but my mind was somewhere else— back at the FOB on my little babies and the potential that they held. *Go ahead and let me die, Lord,* I thought, *but not until I've had the chance to explore those miracle plants.*

The injustice that had kept medical marijuana from people for over 60 years rippled through me once again. It was hard not to get worked up when you cracked a book and discovered the history behind the plant. Cannabis had been used to treat people for a variety of illnesses for more than 2,000 years before they banned it in 1937.

It was one of the most common medicines found in tinctures, and it worked for everything from anxiety and mental disorder to nausea, colds, and flu. To get a read on why cannabis was banned in the first place, I waded through a lot of research.

From what I could gather, between 1600 and 1890,[2] hemp was a gold crop that everyone wanted to grow. It helped build the America we live in today. In 1619 it was actually illegal not to grow it, such was its perceived value in numerous industries. Cannabis was sold openly to anyone that wanted it in pharmacies across the United States until the Mexican influx in 1920.

Pushing an agenda to reduce immigration of Mexicans into America, politicians and other people of importance began a smear campaign against the Mexican plant "marihuana," which was somehow different to the cannabis found in our

---

2   Dr. Malik Burnett, How Did Marijuana Become Illegal in the First Place, http://www.drugpolicy.org/blog/how-didmarijuana-become-illegal-first-place

medicine cabinets. As the 1930s crept in, the end of alcohol prohibition brought another cannabis enemy to the fore: the liquor industry. Then a convergence happened. Other industries experiencing their rise to prominence jumped on the "cannabis is evil" bandwagon. Everyone from the textile industry to the printing industry was ready to see the end of hemp. After all, it threatened their sales. A grotesque campaign of lies bloomed from the mouths of these profiteering hypocrites.

It was the liquor industry that financed that famous movie, *Reefer Madness*. It was a collection of lobbyists that supported marijuana prohibition that began to spread the total lies about it. Some of those lies? Marijuana is the devil's weed. Marijuana turns nice boys into fiends. Marijuana makes white girls sleep with Negros. Marijuana causes violent behavior.

One by one the lies were spread by a propaganda machine, which was owned by people in power. The Marijuana Tax Act of 1937 became the Controlled Substances Act of the 1970s. Nixon would not even entertain that cannabis was a good thing when he was in power. Study after study was suppressed. Americans lost 2,000 years of excellent health to greedy companies.

I cannot blame the state of our health these days on marijuana prohibition alone. But I do believe that it fueled a lot of unhealthy fires—the rise of poisons across many industries and the influx of chemical medicines that do not work as well. Our government and the brightest people in our country supported the death of a crop that made America great.

Future generations will look back on the period between 1920 and 1996 as the most corrupt days in American history.

They turned off the lights, and we all stumbled around in the dark. Now people are paying for this ignorance with their lives. How the hell did we let that happen?

I stole another glance at Mike. I knew there was truth to his pleas that my seeds would never make it back to America. However ridiculous I knew it was, the law was still the law. Unfortunately, it was too late for me. I was already consumed by the idea. Best case scenario, Mike would get rid of the plants himself; worst case, he would turn me in. That or someone with our private contracting firm would cart me off for messing around with "drugs" before I get near a plane.

I did not care. I had found a possible legendary strain that would help people recover from serious illness, and nothing was going to stop me. Garda-World would take me back if I was fired. I had worked for them the previous winter in the Helmand Province on Protection Security Detail. Nobody, and I mean nobody, wanted to work there, especially as a medic.

It was a high-threat Afghan war zone where I had to perform PSD operations and run security for ex-pats and LN guard forces. In other words, I had to protect the USAID boys that were building a large Afghan National Army base just outside of war-ravaged Nad-e-Ali. Nobody wanted us there—not the locals, not the Taliban, and not the kind-faced contract worker that was stacking bricks in your compound. They all wanted you dead and gone.

I had landed up in that place thanks to my first attempt at growing medical marijuana. It did not go well. My basement was damp and the grow was run on a shoestring budget without the shoes. Mold had infested my plants and made them unfit for use. The operation went belly up the moment the mold appeared on the first plant.

I had spent four grueling years in Iraq with the mental

scars to prove it. My only way out was to produce a decent grow to get my mind straight. Instead, I was back in another war zone that same year. Life can be a real donkey kick in the neck sometimes. I do not regret my actions but only that they were not more carefully executed.

My whole life I had been made to suffer with manic, bi-polar, schizophrenic tendencies from the colorful diaspora of men my mother paraded through my fragile childhood. Of course I was not normal; I had never seen what it looked like. War only aggravated my anger. After the tours in Iraq, I was not fit to shovel shit for a few cents an hour.

The world had closed in on me, and I was trapped inside a mind of broken thoughts. The harmony I had been careful to nurture to maintain my sanity in life would pop in and out of focus, like a cruel jack-in-the-box showing me all the regrets of my past. Every now and then I would be faced with a mirror, and could not stand to see the man looking back at me.

PTSD[3] is strange like that. Days go by and things add up, a little reminder here, a flash there.

Eventually it feels like a balloon has inflated inside of your head. All of that pain has to escape somewhere. No one can face the reality of death like that without feeling the annihilating fear that goes with it.

Your nerves are always prickling like thorns pressed against your skin. If something hurts too much, you have to channel the pain somewhere. Sadly, it is usually on the people you love best. Every night is a pantomime of violence that rips your mind apart, and every day the confused logic of that fact is paraded around for everyone to see.

---

3   Post-Traumatic Stress Disorder, http://www.helpguide.org/articles/ptsd-trauma/post-traumaticstress-disorder.htm

I believe it comes from our most primitive side, when man would destroy man simply because of no law and simply because they just could because of anger or resentment. With the introduction of laws and law enforcement, man is forced to dampen those primitive urges to obey the laws. There are some that simply cannot dampen those primitive urges. Which is illogical, not illegal—following the laws or following your primitive urges?

Since my old man had run off with our money when I was a boy, my mind had not been right. I suffered from so many symptoms that I did not even know when I was being paralyzed by a new set of them that had come to fuck with my day. When my grow operation in Michigan began to fail, I decided to start my own paramedical staffing company for the local film and television market. The governor of Michigan gave huge tax incentives to the TV and film industry at that time, so there were a lot of new film industry-related businesses popping up everywhere in Michigan, kind of like the cannabis industry in America right now. Thousands of people threw themselves into the industry in one way or another in hopes of making it in the Hollywood industry.

My ex-wife Roseanna saw an opportunity at Lifton Institute, a new film school that opened up in Allen Park with headquarters in Hollywood, and took advantage of the chance to learn something fun and work in the industry. The class project was to complete a short student film and be graded on it within your choice of skill, whether it be sound, editing, acting, makeup, etc., and hopefully find work. As the filming began, they were able to contract a bright up-and-coming actor, Bren Foster, for the lead role in order to assist everyone else on what it is like to work with a real actor. With some stunts added in, due to the film being based on cage fighting, they needed a medic on the set. I volunteered for Roseanna and the class since I was home at the time and looking for work myself, plus it was another great opportunity for who knows what.

After being on the set a couple weeks, I was asked to take part in a small "role" in the movie. Because of my size, I was asked to take part in a scuffle between Bren and a security guard inside a hallway; I always look the part of the "security guard." After a couple takes of us fighting in the hallway until he killed me for the movie script, we realized we caused a significant amount of damage to the walls. We had a good laugh about it.

Roseanna has more kindness than most anyone I know, and all packed in a 5' blond hair, blue-eyed Irish beauty. She has always been there for me, no matter how hard I made it for her, and our divorce was ultimately a joint decision. She has the biggest heart for animals, and has made some sacrifices for them. Her inner strength is matched to mine.

Roseanna would help me with the new, small LLC business, and it was a great idea. Aside from the fact that no one would hire me due to the economic downturn, I knew I could work for myself in an industry I knew well and make a decent living. Everything was going as planned, until the newly appointed governor decided to take away all the film industry incentives that my entire company was based around.

We watched as our investment washed down the tubes. There was nothing to be done. I sold off as much of the expensive medical equipment as I could and took a major beating on the used ambulance I had just acquired. My dreams of operating a successful paramedical staffing company were over in the blink of an eye.

Our financial situation was darkening, and Roseanna sold her 14k wedding ring I had worked so hard on acquiring with the help of a team buddy in Iraq, Cherry, whose father was an incredible jeweler. We both lost a lot that day, and I will never forget the look on Roseanna's face as we were "happy" to take the $3,500 for it. The feeling you had when you first proposed seems to just wash down the sewer drain and vanish forever.

Also during this same time, Homeland Security was beefing up, and the Border Patrol was hiring. With my military and security background, weapons training, and medical skill, I was a sure win for a position. I passed the written and also the oral interview held at the Dearborn Holiday Inn on Michigan Ave. Out of fourteen people, only two passed, and the family was very excited as this would mean after a background check, I would have the chance to stay home for good and continue to protect my country as a full-time job. When we lost the medical staffing business and everything else, we were forced to seek credit counseling. We were informed to either file bankruptcy or lose everything; we had no choice but to file a Chapter 13 in 2008.

After returning to Iraq a couple months later, I received an email to contact the Homeland Security recruiting office. They informed me over the phone that due to my bankruptcy, I was not fit to work for Homeland Security. When I asked why, she replied that due to my financial hardship in the past, I could be influenced to take bribes at the border. In other words, in America, if you happen to fall on financial hardship, no matter what the cause, your integrity is lost forever. I continued working my job under a secret security clearance the government gave me so I can protect, assist, and even save American lives in the Middle East...but I was not fit to do it in my own homeland?

It was fun while it lasted, though, and I had the opportunity to work (in a very small way) with a few celebrities and see how a movie or TV show was put together. I had the opportunity to work on a number of shows for the HBO series, *Hung*, starring Thomas Jane. In the opening credits, where he is filmed undressing in different parts of Detroit, I was the medic on all of those. It gave me a chance to see Detroit from an outsider's point of view…even a celebrity's, and they all pretty much said the same thing. "Amazing city, amazing potential, amazing disappointment"—and they were all correct.

While working as the set medic for the movie, *Stone*, filmed at Jackson prison, I met Robert De Niro and Edward Norton there. After a few days, the assistant director asked me if I wanted to be in the movie; it seems I had a good look to play a prison guard. I got my 15 seconds when Mila Jovavich was visiting Norton in prison. I was the guard in the window who took her I.D. while she was scanned. I had a great 30-minute conversation with Mila while on break sitting on the grass outside the scene where she meets up with De Niro for the first time and talked about Michigan and Detroit. She was just like an old friend, and it passed the time.

I had tried everything I knew up to that point. The next time I returned home from Iraq for a little R&R, I did not want to go out there again. But that is the irony of war. Once it has you, it tends to stick in your throat like a popcorn kernel. I had tried the grow, starting my own small business, doing a stint in school—anything to be able to stay with my family and keep financially afloat.

My only option after all of that was to get back on the Internet and find an overseas gig in some horrifying place on Earth where I would have to fight for survival. The British company Garda-World was hiring medics and responded in double quick time to my application.

My specific skill set was always in demand. As an American and a medic, with security clearance and WPPS training, there was never a plane headed to anywhere in the world that did not want me on it, but the Middle East always called me back for some reason. That was how I ended up in the godforsaken Helmand Province. Before me, the medic that worked for Garda-World contracted some kind of disease and had to evac home. His ticket back to England was my first ticket to Afghanistan.

I had a family that needed things and a responsibility to get them what they needed. The pay was good, and I needed a job. It was as simple as that to fly back into hell, almost as if I just did not need to think about it, like muscle memory.

The radio crackled next to me, and I was roused from my musings, back in a pinned down position with Matt and Mike. The damn QRF was taking forever. We might have to switch to plan B and get our own sorry asses out of here.

The worst thought was that at any moment the Taliban could have navigated around us and found a clear position of assault. All three of us would be dead before we would have time to relocate. It was best not to have those thoughts at all. Stay alert, but do not let your mind wander too far into fear. Fear gets men killed out here.

Instinctively, I sank back into thoughts about my life, which transported me away from there. With all the cosmic intersections in a person's life, war was definitely one of mine. All three—Kuwait, Iraq, and Afghanistan—were a result of my mother's choice to move us to California. I often wondered if any of this would have happened had I gone with her to Michigan or if my biological father had the strength to raise his own children.

We all make those kinds of choices. It is only later when

we realize the gravity that they had in our lives. When I had stood outside that recruiting office, it could have meant nothing to me. But it did not. My eyes hung on a poster on their wall, listing the requirements for entry. There were not very many, but I had failed one of the important ones.

You had to have a high school diploma or GED to qualify. Even if I had wanted to join then and there, I could not. Hopelessness churning in my stomach along with the sample food, I headed back outside into the general nowhere. I was lost and scared, afraid of a life on the street without any hope of safety. Overwhelmed, a new question crossed my mind.

How do I get a GED? My feet carried me towards a phone booth later that night. I needed to seek council, to find a platform I could build on. I called my mom. It was very early in the Michigan morning when I called, around three or four to be sure. I hoped that she would accept the charges and answer the call. There was no certainty that she would.

The phone rang in time with each nervous breath that I swallowed. Then the click of life. On hearing my mother's voice, tears blossomed from me like they never had before. I recounted the past few days and months, soaked in my own emotions. She listened patiently as I said to her, "Hi, Mom, I'm really glad you picked up. I know it's not the best timing, but I thought you would want to know that I decided I want to get my GED and go into the military."

I was told to go to the nearest Greyhound bus station, where a ticket would be waiting for me. I could come and stay with her in Michigan while I got my GED. The two days I waited there without eating a thing seemed to pass by with sheer joy. There was a great sense of relief and a palpable moment of happiness between us when our eyes met at the station after the long ride there. That happy reunion lasted for several days.

Then the elation wore off, and it was back to dodging the new stepfather and staying away from home as much as possible. I worked hard on getting my GED, though, and with the possibility of boot camp ahead of me, I started to run every day and work out with anything I could grab and use. I would say that it was like caveman cross-fit. I knew when I had said it to my mom that I had meant it. When I finally took the test, I was satisfied with my answers. Soon after that, I got the letter saying that I had passed.

The minute I had proof of my GED, I made my way to the nearest recruiting office. It was one of those combo operations with all four branches of the service represented. There were four colorful doors that welcomed me inside, each brandishing a smart branch logo with uniformed recruiters waiting to help.

These guys always looked like vultures to me, swooping down on unsuspecting people trying to hook them into something nobody wanted to do. As soon as you offer yourself to them willingly, they descend on you like a rotten carrion. I decided to keep an open mind about it, and I would keep it simple and just listen to the first person that talked to me.

An Air Force guy was the first to lock eyes with me, but it was the Navy recruiter that aggressively intercepted my stroll and engaged me in conversation. "Hey there. How's it going?" I pretended to be surprised at his introduction and shook his hand. "Anything I can do to help you?"

"Sure. I was thinking about signing up."

"Great! Come into my office, and let's get acquainted."

We exchanged pleasantries for a few minutes, then a short test was placed in front of me to see where I would fit. The recruiter grabbed my work and ducked around the corner; not too long after, he returned with a smile. "You did pretty good; in fact, right now we only seem to have two choices for you." This was music to my ears. I had gone from being on the street and having no choices to a glowing two.

He told me I could either choose the medical field route or take the nuclear submarine route. Apparently, I was supposed to be thrilled with either choice, but I had no change in tempo. I had no idea what either field meant, and he saw it. "I can make it easier for you if you like," he said to me, still beaming. "Let me break it down to you like this: In a nuclear submarine, 60 guys go down, and soon after, 30 couples come back up." I thought it was a pretty lame joke, but I went with it since he seemed to think it was hysterical. We both enjoyed a hearty laugh together.

"The medical field is full of girls," he added after that. To this day, I am not sure if he was being helpful or if he just had a quota to fill, but his argument was compelling. I did not have to linger on the two prospects for very long. I agreed to join the medical field, where I would meet a lot of girls and have a solid understanding of what having a future actually feels like, and I signed on the dotted line.

It was January 1990, and I had finally done something worth doing. My mom was very proud of me. I was en route to a nearby Military Entrance Processing Station and feeling on top of the world. Since traveling from California, I never really added to my wardrobe, so I flopped off the bus and into fourteen inches of snow in Great Lakes, Illinois. I had a pair of board shorts and a long sleeve t-shirt. Master Chief began telling me in his own way how incredibly stupid I was and how lucky I was to have him as both my parents for the next few vacation weekends there before I would have a career in the military.

CHAPTER 5

BOOT CAMP SURVIVAL

"By any of the major criteria of harm—mortality, morbidity, toxicity, addictiveness and relationship with crime—cannabis is less harmful than any of the other major illicit drugs, or than alcohol or tobacco."
REPORT OF THE BRITISH POLICE FOUNDATION, MARCH 2000

The moment I met my first ever Master Chief, he had nothing nice to say about my appearance. It seemed like everything about me irked him, but I was soon to discover that this was nothing more than the way of the Navy. I was not in sunny California or lazy Michigan anymore. This was middle-of-winter Illinois Navy Boot Camp.

I was a fast learner, to my credit. I learned that to click along in relative comfort, I had to speak clearly and loudly while doing exactly what Master Chief said. Otherwise, he would be two inches from my face screaming obscenities, and no one can tolerate that for very long. Military boot camp has a way of forcing you to comply that works.

My first few days rained down on me in a hail of screaming followed closely by a relentless barrage of medical exams. After the tests were done, we had to submit to a plethora of shots, old fashioned needle and the new air gun injection, which surprisingly feel a lot worse than they sound. The medics continually shouted, "Keep moving forward. Do not move when being injected."

What? Don't move where? A guy ahead of me in line, 6' 6" and 275+ moved a little while they were trying to inject him with the needleless air gun and ended up with a four-inch horizontal laceration about 1-1/2 inches deep into his arm. Everyone came up off the floor when he hit full force and passed out. "Move forward!"

There were three more guys in line that were immediately ill, throwing up all over the place. I was the only one in line that was not too fazed by the shots. Unfortunately, they were not done with me. I had a bad reaction to the yellow fever shot and became completely jaundiced, turning yellow all over and sweating bullets.

You could easily tell the new recruits from the seasoned ones. Whenever you see a platoon marching in painful unison all with a limp to the same side, you know they just arrived and just received their bacilli shot. It felt like a golf ball was shoved into your upper left ass-cheek.

I got so sick that I lost the ability to walk, and my temperature rose so high that the doctor ordered the entire squad to heave me—mattress and all—from the top bunk where I lay over to the showers so that I could cool off. I was lifted and roughly carried in my yellow delirium to the shower floor, where the cold water was unceremoniously turned on and I was left there to recover. Twice.

I am not ashamed to say that I barely survived. That damn

yellow fever shot nearly killed me. Once I had recovered from the shots, boot camp began. It was as expected. A lot of orders, a lot of toeing the line. After boot camp, I got stationed at the Great Lakes, where I attended school for Hospital Corpsman. It was an interesting and riveting time.

A large amount of information had to be crammed into my thick skull, and I worked hard to get it all in during that short period of time. The days peeled away like old car stickers, and soon I found myself stationed at the Oakland Naval Hospital in Northern California. It was the best place for a corpsman to find their legs.

All around me was postcard scenery and gorgeous California women. I was a Navy man now, with all the respect and integrity that a uniformed man deserved. As a young, healthy guy, I took advantage of everything the Bay area had to offer me. I had been given a second chance at a better life, and I was miles away from the kid who had been thrown in jail for stealing a comforter. I knew that bigger things were in my immediate future.

Over the next several months, I worked in different areas of the hospital, learning the ropes. There was the ICU, CCU, pre- and post-surgical, and the ER unit. With my natural affinity for excitement, I found that I was best in an emergency. They told me I had a real talent for keeping a cool head in the face of total chaos.

I made friends with a handful of corpsmen I met at the hospital, and we would hang out together on weekends, having fun and being young. This was where I met Bryan, who became my best friend in the corps. Bryan came from a giant family of about 10 siblings, and because of that, he grew up without the finer things in life.

Accustomed to being poor, he struck me immediately as

a trustworthy guy who was good with people. He certainly seemed to love his family a whole lot. I both admired and envied that in him, having gone without any kind of real family support my whole life. So the two of us fell in together like kindred spirits do.

Bryan dated an RN from the hospital at the time, and she had a pretty hot sister, so the four of us ended up being a temporary family. The girl's sister and I spent a lot of time exploring the San Francisco Bay area together. It was some of the happiest years of my life. I learned to grow up and had fun doing it.

At the same time, I put my childhood behind me. One of the ways I did this was that I learned how to drink. Not the crap liquor and beer that I drank in high school but the hard stuff—the stuff meant for military men. I learned to never set foot in a bar without leaving completely out of my mind drunk with happiness and alcohol.

While stationed at Oakland, Saddam Hussein invaded Kuwait, and the military began to increase their asset hold in the Middle East out of necessity. It was the time leading up to the Gulf War, and tensions were rippling through the base. A day came when Bryan and I headed into the PX on base and noticed a small poster tacked to the entrance door.

Turns out, the Marines were looking for volunteers. The poster read, "Jump to the green side!" The two of us stopped to read the fine print on the poster and realized what it was. With the Gulf War only moments from realization, the Marines needed more field medics. Our minds full of idealistic notions of war, Bryan and I headed into the PX.

By the time we left that day, both of us were rearing to go green. Yes, we were young, stupid, independent, and on a mission to prove something to the world. We both always held a high confidence level. The poster had spoken about a need to pass a rigorous, highly intensive fitness test, so we immediately hit the gym. In addition to weight lifting and heavy core exercises, we also jogged, ran sprints, and did whatever else we could think of to get our bodies into marathon shape.

We spent a month working on our fitness levels, and then we were ready to undergo the rigorous fitness test to see if we could go green. There were several different components to the test, and Bryan whipped right through them. I had spent a lot of time in the ocean and outdoors, so I figured it would be a breeze for me too.

But I flunked one of the tests. Luckily, I was given a second chance the following day and managed to squeak through with a pass. By the time the two of us had passed our tests, the initial invasion of Iraq had begun. Bryan and I both went full Marine regulation, a choice we proudly made. Soon we were in a mini boot camp for field medical training.

After countless blistering weeks of breaking our balls, we were assigned to the Light Armored Infantry Battalion. They stuck us on a plane with our gear, and we said goodbye to America. Bound for Kuwait, we were to meet up with the 1st Recon Light Armored Vehicle Division there. It was all a wonderful and terrifying adventure.

The flight was the longest one I have stored in my memory. Bryan and I sat across from each other, talking for hours. We learned a lot about our lives from the past and grew to appreciate our roots a little more. Even though we were young, we spoke of death like it was an old friend. I believe I promised to look after Bryan's family if he died in combat.

Looking back, we were so young and naïve, so full of the excitement and ego of war that we never stopped to think about where we were going or what it might do to us if we survived. No one gets out of combat zones as alive as they were when they first got there. We disembarked from the plane in an entirely new country and were taken from the tarmac to a large battalion aid station that had been set up nearby.

Straight from the plane and into a combat aid station set up somewhere in the middle of nowhere it seemed and with ailing, dying, and bleeding soldiers, we were told to help in any way that we could until our own unit could arrange for our transport. So that was what we did for the first week in Iraq. Bryan and I helped take care of the wounded or sick personnel that were brought into the triage and the emergency room.

The emergency room helped anyone that needed it. We had military expats, local nationals, and civilians that had all been casualties of the bloody Iraq invasion. There were a lot of children that had become victims of the genocide. Many children meant many grieving parents, and so we became accustomed to the rattling sobs and grief-stricken moans of the triage tent. It was a lot to take in for two new medics.

Civilians were kept separate from the military personnel, and they were placed under constant security watch. Some of the things that we witnessed were comical; some of the things were heart wrenching. There was one cheerful army soldier who was in serious traction with two broken legs, the result of an accidental fall. In fact, I believe a majority of the injuries during the Kuwait Liberation War were of our own doing.

We called him "Fall Guy" because he had a tough name to remember. He was one of the luckier ones. They sent him off for surgery in Germany and then home to recover. Then there was a Kuwaiti woman with a daughter who had been severely burned due to an explosion inside her village. The burns were so bad that I held little hope for her recovery.

The mother was very young herself and strikingly pretty. She came over to me one day and asked in her own way if I could help her. There was nothing I could do but empathize with her. I did not know the language, which made me feel very distant and unable to help, but the more I tried to tell her nothing could be done, the more she pleaded for help. I had dozens of other patients in need of urgent medical attention, but she looked so helpless.

Exasperated, she looked at me and in broken English said, "Please, please, sir, help me, my friend."

I gave in and followed her to her daughter. She was lying in bed behind a curtain, and the violent smell of burnt human flesh and hair made me gag. It immediately reminded me of the time when one of my live-in enforcers decided to do away with an old dog I brought home when I was around 13 years old. I thought it needed a home, so I made it a bed and two bowls for food and water out back. He complained about it for four days until he found a way to get rid of it entirely. I thanked him for it and never looked at another animal the same since. I forced myself to sit down on the bed with the frail little girl, and I took her hand in my own.

I looked at the young mother, who had settled across from me. I was worried that she wanted me to do something more, something I just could not provide. But that was exactly it. She did not ask me to come as a medic to do "medical" stuff. She just wanted someone to comfort her daughter, to let her know everything was going to be all right. I was not told this; it was just easily implied. We sat there for a time, me holding her daughter's hand as her uneasiness and lack of comfort seemed to have calmed down.

The girl lay on her stomach, with her head towards me and her eyes closed. She had several IV lines running off her arm and was pretty doped up. That is the only way someone can exist when they are that far gone. Her face was about 50% burnt, along with most of her chest all the way down her legs to her toes. I do not even want to explain the other injuries. She was running right into it when a shell hit the dirt.

I must have been there for three hours with the girl and her mother. No one seemed to need me as chaos ran like a roller coaster in the main hallway. The flight medics eventually came in with a nurse and explained that they were flying her to a hospital better equipped for this type of injury. I helped get her ready. All the while, her mother just sat there by my side, watching.

When the medics came for the girl, they wheeled her out into the narrow hallway along with a few other patients. There were four gurneys waiting on the tarmac ready for airlift. As we stood there, the daughter opened her eyes a little—not as someone who had been asleep but as someone that had been awake the entire time. She looked at me and smiled without moving a muscle. Even though she probably could not speak if she wanted to, she did not have to.

When they were ready, a group of flight medics took them away. The mother followed them; she would be going on the bird as well. I stood there for a second or two and watched them go. Then I was called back into the fray.

Bryan and I were assigned from one medical location to another that first week, plugging any holes that the military had exposed. Word eventually came down from the 1st Recon LAV that they were pulling back for repairs and additional logistics. It turned out, there was only enough room for one additional medic at the tip of the spear somewhere. One of us—it did not matter which—would have to meet up with one of the platoons. The other would have to stay behind and wait for the next chance to rendezvous. It was not the news we wanted to hear, but it was news. I could see that Bryan wanted it bad, even more than I did. The open desert was calling to him. He was a great medic but more of a hard charger than me—a devil doc who just wanted to get out there and get dirty.

Bryan had never been cut out for the closed quarters Band-Aid stuff. I assessed the matter and grabbed two insulin syringes from a nearby table. I palmed them and placed my hands behind my back. "One of these is 1cc; the other is 2cc. Whoever picks the smaller one gets to go sand surfing." Bryan was up for the game and ready to pick. Bryan considered his options and picked an arm. When he got the 1cc syringe, I quickly threw the other one into our Sharps Container to show him how upset I was. That we only had 1cc insulin syringes went right over Bryan's head. Like I said, the kid was not really cut out for the indoor stuff.

At the end of it all, I was happy to let him get the post. He deserved the opportunity, and one would come around for me soon enough.

The two of us had been stationed in these big bunk-house style tents while on the base. That night we stayed up all night, talking. When 0400 hours came around the next morning, Bryan kitted up and headed out. We said our goodbyes as best we knew how. I watched as he climbed into a Blackhawk and took off. It took about 30 minutes of waiting around on the tarmac for that to happen. When it did, I felt a sense of grief. I never did see him again after that. Another good friend gone forever. I slunk back to my bunk with a heavy heart and an all too familiar feeling swishing around in my stomach. I never told anyone that I did that for Bryan; it was simply an unconditional single selfless act given to a well deserving human being. An honorable unmention.

I had a bad habit of losing friends. They just never seemed to stick around for too long. This did not prevent me from feeling good about my decision. Bryan deserved the shot at open combat in Iraq. He wanted it more than anything, and I was glad to give it to him. Sacrificing for others has always been a big part of my life. I never needed the recognition; it was fulfilling enough as it was.

Maybe that is just who I am. Either way, I had a feeling that war would show me what I was made of before the end. There was no hiding from it in this place. I still struggle to put myself ahead of other people, but that made me a damn good medic. Morals and ethics were evolving at an incredible pace, and I was proud of what I had already accomplished and where I could go from there.

Later that week, I was still in a somber mood from losing Bryan to the sandbox. As I was getting dressed one morning, a young officer strode smartly into my tent and called out my name. "Yes sir?" I responded, surprised. He walked over to my bunk and delivered some sobering news. Word had come down the chain of command that Bryan had taken the only available field medic slot. I would not be deploying as planned.

I was to be shipped to our Oakland-based hospital ship, the USNC Mercy, along with a select number of other medical personnel at the base. They seemed to need our tent for something more demanding. I cannot say that I was not disappointed. I wanted to earn the right to say that I had served in combat, a dream that every military man has from the early days of boot camp.

Within 48 hours I was on the same ship that most of my medical peers had taken to war, and we cruised the Persian Gulf waters for the next few months working exclusively for the crew. It eventually became clear that there were no positions to fill in Kuwait and less space for me in the desert, so I continued my float on the Mercy, and I was sent back to base.

The Mercy departed for home in March, and I arrived back in Oakland on April 23, 1991. I enjoyed another six months of partying and total boredom, which flashed by like a lightning streak. Then one day, something new happened. The great Oakland Hills fire hit, and the call went out for all medical personnel and volunteers to immediately dispatch. I was on the first bus out.

The Great Oakland Hill's Fire practically engulfed the Warren Freeway. When I arrived, the Battalion Aid Station was still being erected. The freeway itself was shut down, so I helped set up the tent with everyone else. There, on the highest level of a clover leaf freeway overpass, we started taking in people the second the equipment was inside.

A giant tent in the middle of the road, with the skies outside blazing orange and black, flickering as the smoke drifted by…it was like a scene from a movie. Nothing in my life up to that point prepared me for what I was about to see, not even the triage tent back in Iraq. We were 60 feet up in the air, and with the aid station done and additional logistics still coming in, I jogged to the overpass to check out the fire. There was a 360 degree view, and everything was burning. Heat emanated off every surface, like it had risen up out of hell itself. The entire world was glowing red, and we were in the center of it. A moment later, once I was back in the tent, chaos struck. Firefighters and other emergency staff were pouring into the tent from all directions, mobbing the place.

One by one I was handed injured people and animals in quick succession. There was not a moment to breathe, to stop, or to take stock of the situation. Some were not seriously hurt, while others reminded me of the girl back in Iraq. They would be lucky to survive the night. As it wore on and the heat intensified, people and animals just kept coming.

Each time a firefighter walked into the tent, thick plumes of smoke clung to them like they had stepped inside a dragon's mouth. This was my first introduction to what it meant to be a firefighter. I watched as men with courage left to battle the blaze and saw their emotional state on their return. I learned to respect firefighters that evening.

I felt like a man born into a new career through a literal trial by fire. Early the next year, I was sent south to Camp Pendleton attached to the 1st Recon LAV Platoon. I was put through an even more rigorous combat field medical training course, and my skills improved. As the months trailed by, I heard various rumors about Bryan.

There was a rumor that the 1st Recon's LAV Infantry Battalion medic had been badly wounded or even killed in the war. Then there was another that said Bryan had been sent to Force Recon. I kept thinking I would run into him at some point, but I never did. Eventually, I stopped hearing rumors, and all leads went cold.

At Camp Pendleton, Area 21, Camp Del Mar was my official station, although, at the time, a handful of medics were bouncing around from company to company. We would go from Alpha, to Bravo, then Charlie, depending on who needed a medic and for what mission. Occasionally I worked at the local battalion aid station on sick call.

If there was ever a new mission or operation being offered, I was always the first to volunteer for it. I even attended a two-week basic laboratory course when I first developed my interest in biology and science. Those were laid back days, where I did not have to worry about anything but my career in the military.

I was young and bursting with energy—the kind that made me the medic who would walk backwards up the hill on a 20-mile hump in full pack, shouting at my Marines to do better. "C'mon, guys, keep it going! Keep it going!" When we stopped to take a break and let our aching feet breathe, I was still running around making sure everyone was okay, checking their feet and making sure the water intake was sufficient. The life of a medic!

Then I would be back at the front of the formation, encouraging everyone to move out again. I took good care of those boys. It is a fundamental truth that when a Marine platoon respects their medic, that medic will never have to pay for his own drinks when he is out with his brothers. That is how it was back in those days. I drank for free.

Grunts were trained to cover the radioman, watch their officer's six, and get in good with their medic. It was sage advice. I clicked with a select group of guys pretty quickly, and every weekend we would hit the town, painting one end of San Diego to the other a cheeky rouge then all the way down through the main strip of Tijuana.

One of my buddies at the time was named Ski. He was very into the new underground house music scene and began taking us all to these secret parties called "raves." He had brought flyers back to the base one day, detailing where all the hottest underground parties would be up and down the West Coast.

He mentioned once how the scene was particularly awesome in LA right now, so we decided to check it out.

The party turned out to be in the basement of some huge building slap bang in the middle of downtown LA. For the first time, someone offered me ecstasy. I asked Ski what it was, and he said not to worry about it. "Trust me. You won't regret it," he said as he was moving back to the dance floor with two beautiful little raver girls. For the first time, I decided it would be okay to take it. You never forget your first time on that drug. Everyone around me was having the time of their lives, and so was I.

That night my life changed forever. I was hooked on the music, the parties, and, for the first time, the drugs too. It was the beginning of the California desert rave scene, where parties would be held on Indian reservations, where the law did not matter. Every weekend became every night; it seemed the party would never end.

CHAPTER 6

EPIC PARTIES AND DUTY

"We have been terribly and systematically misled [about cannabis] for nearly 70 years in the United States."

DR. SANJAY GUPTA

Being in the military was a barbed, two-way road. You had a lot of rules that you had to live by, but you regularly delighted in breaking them. After all, we were just a bunch of young guys who were starting out in life, and there were few things a uniform could do to suppress that kind of bold energy. Pushing boundaries happened naturally.

Our superiors even understood that rule-breaking was part of the job. One Sunday night, on a particularly alcohol-sodden party evening, my roommate and I decided it would be best not to let the two intoxicated girls we had met drive such a long way home. So we decided to bring these two girls back to our room at the bunkhouse.

It seemed like the right thing to do. We were too drunk to drive them all the way home, and no one wanted the party to end anyways.

Having "guests" in the bunkhouse was strictly off limits. To us, that meant if we got caught, we would be in for it. By no means did it mean that we should not actually bring girls back to our room. At least that is what your drunken brain tells you at four in the morning. When reveille sounded at dusk, we were all still passed out from the activities of the previous evening.

Waking up late and startled, we had to report for duty right away. We decided to leave the girls hidden in the bunkhouse. They would remain quiet while we carried out our duties, and once we got off, we would create an extraction plan. As we filed into formation directly in front of our bunkhouse, two men from the inspection squad marched unceremoniously and directly to my room, knocked loudly, and went inside.

Standing at attention, we were powerless to help the girls. All we could do was watch the scene unfold. Stealing glances at the third floor window of our bunks, we saw the men milling about in our room. The women appeared with them a moment later. Shortly after that, the whole lot of them came marching back out into the chilly morning.

My Gunny watched as the inspection team marched the women across the lawn and into another building. I had never seen him that angry before, and it was directed at me. What followed was the loudest and most frightening speech I had ever heard. It was violent and fueled with fury, and it was done in front of our entire platoon. Finally, after what seemed like hours of verbal abuse, he dismissed the platoon and screamed at me to meet him in his office within the next five minutes. Already crestfallen and close to shaking from the furious drilling, I made my way over to his office, expecting the worst. Was he going to dishonorably discharge me from service?

"Close the fucking door!" he shouted as I entered.

My stomach had become the universe, and I was falling into it. I stood at attention, holding my breath.

Then he laughed. "Damn, Doc, you need two women? At least you could have gotten them out to the bus stop at the front gate before sunrise. Now, have you learned your lesson?"

The tension snapped in half immediately. I was off the hook. Gunny sat me down and told me about the stupid things he had done when he was in my position. He told me that actions like that had to be met with discipline and that he had no choice but to vilify me in front of the men. I was the medic and a role model to everyone. I had to become his example.

At the same time, he told me not to take it to heart and that it was nothing personal. That was just the way of the military. Most everyone breaks the rules, but if you are caught, you are in hot water. I saw Gunny in a whole new light that day. I knew that he was just doing his job, toughening us up for situations far worse than these.

I had no idea that Gunny Procop was a normal human being before that day. He played the necessary role so that he could keep a bunch of disobedient kids in line long enough to do their duty. You had to respect that. I was a solid medic with a company of well-respected men. We worked hard every day and never ignored the duty we had to each other.

I took care of my Marines on the field and off it. Gunny knew the responsibilities that we faced called for some shenanigans while we were still ripe for them. Soon we could be off to fight a war we knew little about. I was just a young, stupid punk back then trying to fit in with the angle of things. Our life then was about the parties and the duty.

During these explosive partying years, I developed a keen addiction to the music scene and eventually found myself roaming the record shops, where I started listening to vinyl. I bought mix tapes and found myself thinking back to the days when I lived in Detroit when the Wizard on WJLB was a big deal. I got so into it that I bought a turntable and a small mixer and started a new passion of mine—DJing.

I would create my own mix tapes up in the barracks and even managed to sell some of my tapes at a few of the record stores in the area. I played small house parties to begin with, but they got bigger as I got better. I became so good that I landed my own booking agent, and I was heating up in the local music scene. Times were so great that I decided to leave the military.

I had been a soldier for four years and figured that it was enough. I would use my VA school money to become a doctor. I had always played with the idea of going into medicine full time, and the decision seemed right. With my military guidance counselor's help, I applied to the School of Medicine at several colleges.

Because my mother still lived in Michigan at the time, I was careful to include the University of Michigan on that list. Word came down that Michigan had accepted me, and I made arrangements to go to live with her while I settled into school there. Since joining the military, I had been in regular contact with my mother on a weekly basis.

I knew she was single, which was a big deciding factor for me. Having one of her "father of the year" characters there would not fly for me this time. Just as well—with my military training, I probably would have ended up in jail for murder if she had been with another Sid or Don. I was excited to be a freshman studying medicine, and with that in mind, I left the military.

An honorable discharge they call it. You can come back at any time if you like. With everything set, I packed what I could fit into my car and headed east from Camp Pendleton. Once again, I was leaving everyone I knew behind. It was February of 1994, and new horizons stretched out in front of me. I could do anything!

A lot of the men had saved some of their service money, and I was no different. I had some stashed away from my stint overseas, but the pay had been pathetic, so it was not much. I got into my car and dropped some LSD. It took me two days and two nights straight, but I drove direct from San Diego to Detroit. I did not sleep once during the drive; I did not need to.

The LSD had given me a new kind of energy and focus that made the time streak by in a dozen rainbows colliding with each other along the road. Only one negative thought kept pecking at my insides. What the fuck am I doing? Why am I going back home to live with my mother? Those had been the worst years of my life.

I guess when you are young and impulsive, change happens whether you want it to or not. I always had to follow my heart. If it called me back home and to med school, then so be it. Nothing else mattered. I was a man now, and I controlled what happened to me. Looking back, I would not alter that course. I had places to go and a life to discover.

I arrived at my mom's place in Michigan that same February. She had been working as the manager of a small apartment complex in Redford on the east side of Telegraph, in Detroit Proper. She lived in a comfortable two-bedroom apartment and had cleared out one of the rooms just for me. I bought a bedroom set and settled into the spare room.

I had two goals for myself there in Detroit. One was to broaden my musical knowledge and get to know the amazing DJ scene. The other was to become a doctor. I never feel like I am taking too much on, and I always enjoy the challenge. The first thing I unpacked was my set of turntables, which I placed lovingly on top of my dresser. It felt right to be back with my mom, out of the military, and with prospects again.

My mother was very happy to have me home and supported me from the moment I arrived. I was very lucky to have such a caring lady in my life. It had been ages since the trauma and trials that her men had put us through back in California, but I had the common sense to never bring it up. Neither did she. Those bad memories belonged in the past.

The two of us rubbed along pleasantly together, and things were mostly good. One element of my mother's life that had changed was her new fascination with smoking grass. I had done my fair share of sedating and drug use, but she smoked nonstop. Truth be told, I did not like it. I gave her a hard time about it. It was like weed had replaced men in her life.

Back then I thought of weed as anyone else did—a dangerous drug that the government warned everybody against. It makes you crazy in the end. That is what we were told. I would only find out many years later how wrong I was. My mother had been using it as a sedative to treat her anxiety, PTSD, and other emotional issues. She was right to do so.

Scientifically speaking, cannabis is first and foremost a medicine. Sure, you can use it recreationally, but its strength lies in the 104[4] active cannabinoids found in different strains

---

4   R. Sam Barclay, The Science of Medical Marijuana: What's the Latest?, http://www. healthline.com/

of the plant. Marijuana even led to the discovery of a new system in the human body, the endocannabinoid[5] system, or endogenous cannabinoid system. This system is instrumental in regulating brain chemistry and the body's immune system. The discovery led to some major breakthroughs in medical science back in the '80s that still continue to this day. One thing we have learned is that cannabis is uniquely in tune with the human body, as if we evolved along with it.

Thanks to this system, cannabinoids can positively influence brain chemistry, combating a number of neurological and auto-immune diseases. The cannabinoids act on different receptors in the brain and can combat inflammation, pain, and a huge variety of other disease-causing factors. I did not know it yet, but deep down, I think my mom did.

She smoked often and deeply. Otherwise, it was the usual bustling drama that went along with being an apartment manager. People would come and go at all hours of the day and night, and my mom was always pleasant to everyone and helped in any way she could. Her personality was still there. My only consolation was that this time there was no drunkard taking up space in my kitchen, waiting for a chance to beat the shit out of me.

I began my basic college requirement classes at the University of Michigan in March 1994. My future was bright, and I would often fantasize about becoming the next in-demand trauma surgeon, working at a prestigious hospital. My two introductory courses would surely give me a snapshot of what to expect in medicine as the path stretched out before me.

---

5   Martin A. Lee, The Discovery of the Endocannabinoid System, http://www.beyondthc.com/wp-content/uploads/2012/07/eCBSystemLee.pdf

Within a matter of weeks, I was suffering from extreme boredom and going out of my mind. For hours at a time, I would stare at the expansive white walls and the crystal white fluorescent lights that were dotted above me, longing for escape. As I stared, I saw the next eight years of my life tick by, second by second, moment by moment, just like this.

I felt like I was in some kind of torture chamber and there was no escape. The irony was that I was going to incur a massive student loan debt to do it! Paying to be driven insane…paying to be driven insane. The boredom eventually caught up with me. Even if I managed to make it through the next 2,920 days, my reward would be to work inside a hospital.

More white walls. More fluorescent lights. What the hell had I been thinking? Finally, one day my brain rebelled against my own impulsive stupidity. I stood, a mixture of panic and adrenaline rushing through my veins, and I bolted from the classroom. It was time for a reality check. Dreams are great, but if they make you unhappy, you need to reassess them. Things in your mind are rarely what they are in the real world.

I needed an alternative career path, and I needed it quick. Screw becoming a doctor. Turns out, I was exactly like Bryan. I had to work outdoors, and I had to be where the action was. Why hadn't I seen it before? By the end of May of that year I had dropped out of the University of Michigan. I was never going to sentence myself to a life locked inside a hospital. I still had to complete all of my basic courses, so I signed up for Henry Ford Community College. I figured that it would give me time to decide what I wanted to do with the rest of my life. I was worried that stopping school altogether would derail my progress, and I could not let that happen. I had to take a hard look at the man I wanted to be and make a decision.

As I thought about my childhood, I understood that a large part of me would always care for other people and would want to help them as best I could. Try as I might, I could not shake my natural talent for the medical field; it just seemed like a natural fit. If I added it together with all of the intensive training I got in the military, I had some options.

After some sleepless nights, I decided that I would try my hand at being a paramedic. It would keep me outdoors, and I was a star at high pressure situations when everyone else was losing it. Surely I should use these gifts to save lives.

Paramedics are taught to deal with fast-paced situations that cause trauma in the average person. They see a lot of disturbing things, and lose a lot of lives along the way. In many instances, being a paramedic is not unlike being a military medic except no one is directly trying to kill you. The danger is almost always on the person you are trying to save. In my opinion, this makes paramedics people worthy of respect.

I attended Henry Ford for enough credit hours to receive my EMT- Paramedic certificate. Once I was qualified, I secured my first job working for a private ambulance company. The pay was terrible, and I quickly realized that despite my military training and paramedic qualifications, I would never be well off in that position. Paramedics are so poorly paid that you are forced to live with the lower echelons of American society.

It was either survive with nothing or get a second job. So I started my second job working part time in a retail clothing store at the mall. The mall was a fun place to work, and it gave me the down time I needed from the high stress dailies involved with paramedic practice. While I worked at the clothing store, I became friends with my manager. She was best friends with a gorgeous Mexican girl, and she introduced us one day while I was working my shift. Carmen worked just around the corner from our store at Saks Fifth Avenue. We clicked right away, which was a big surprise for me. I thought that with all of my baggage, finding such a great partner would be a challenge.

I still lived with a Marine mindset and was transitioning from a military man into the civilian career that I believed would suit me best. I had spent four years as a soldier, and you cannot just drop that kind of discipline or aura, especially when it has been drilled into you more ways than one. To help this along, I went in the opposite direction with my appearance.

Always a balls-out kind of guy, I grew out my hair and added a long, curling goatee to my look. I pierced my right eyebrow and both ears, inserting plugs so that they stood out. I wore a skullcap 90% of the time. Along with my baggy clothes and my backpack, which I permanently clung to, I looked more like a hustler than an ex- military man.

Carmen and I dated, and one day she decided that it was time for me to meet her parents. Looking like a total street punk, I agreed and followed Carmen to her strict Mexican Catholic household. To say the meeting was strained would be polite. I was obviously not the kind of man that these devout Catholics wanted for their little girl.

Everything from my buffed out muscles to my pierced ears seemed to offend them. Once I had left, Carmen's dad asked her what the hell had been in my eye. He had never come across an eyebrow bolt before and would not dare ask me what it was. I must have seemed very intimidating, although that was never my intention.

A paramedic with a second job in retail and a military background was startling enough without someone looking like me entering their religious circle. I would have loved to have heard what they said about me to Carmen after that first meeting. I knew that it was not good.

Being in Detroit again aroused my love of the music scene. It was not long before I discovered where the best dance music was happening in the city. The places to be were St. Andrew's, The Shelter, and 3 Floors of Fun, all encased in one brick building. This was where the latest, hottest, and best tracks were being played for miles around. More than anything, I wanted a shot at DJing at one of these smoking locations.

After going there a few times, I was properly introduced to the Detroit electronic music scene by such artists as Mike Huckaby, Sneaky Pete (who became a very good friend of mine), Brian Gillespie, BMG, DJ Godfather, Ritchie Hawtin and John Acquaviva (Canada), and even The Wizard, Jeff Mills. There was an endless number of pure talent who helped build the foundation of the Detroit electronic music scene back then. I was in absolute awe. I introduced myself to the manager at the time, Mike, gave him a copy of one of my recent mixes, and asked him if they were hiring DJs. "We don't need DJs," he said to me, "but we do need a bouncer." It was clear that my muscles were more valuable to him than my musical talent, so I took the gig. It was a chance to be closer to the music anyway.

The pay was decent, and it would help me pay for my vinyl habit, which was not a cheap habit to have. Back then, vinyl cost an absolute fortune, and I had never been particularly good with money. I started bouncing for the club that same evening.

Being a bouncer was a new experience for me. There was always some pain in the ass drunk person to deal with, but the parties and girls made it all worth it. For about two glorious years, I was a bouncer at this club. I was backstage when a lot of the best bands came through the place, and I had a chance to meet them all.

Every Friday night Dennis White promoted Charm Farm, which was also the name of his band that played when he was not spinning records. Sometimes I would hang out with them after the bar closed and always had a blast. Many years later Dennis became the world class DJ, Static Revenger. One Sunday night on 89x during "Big Sonic Heaven" (an old radio show once a week that played new and unique music), my buddy Tolly Marcus played one of the most beautiful tracks I have ever heard, called "Sweetest Day." I pulled over and called him at the station and asked who that song was by. He said, "Control Freq, who is also Static Revenger." I was completely surprised. "You mean Dennis White from Charm Farm?" Nice. That song ended up in both of my weddings. (Thank you, ladies!)

Then one night a huge burling brawl broke out on the main dance floor. A bottle tore through the smoky, light-rippled darkness and hit me at top speed in the head. Blood spouted from the collision, but I was so amped up that I did not notice it at all. I swam through the crowd of people towards the trouble, where the other bouncers were already engaged in the fight.

A few drunken assholes had caused problems and needed to be removed by several of us all at once. Alcohol has the uncanny ability to make even a small man powerfully strong and dangerously aggressive. We fought for 15 minutes before we managed to heave them out of the double front doors and onto the pavement outside.

I was so full of adrenaline that I was not ready to let the fight die. I wanted to continue beating them outside, but a friend had noticed my head wound and dragged me back inside to the bar. There, I was given a towel to try to stop the considerable bleeding. "You all right?" asked the bartender.

"Yeah, but I'm about done with this drunk ass bull shit." I was angry and tired of being a bouncer.

"Every time they come in here, they start a fight," he continued.

"Who are they anyway?" I asked, folding the bloody towel in two.

"Mainly a guy named Kid Rock and his fucking entourage. Just some white idiot selling shitty rap music out of his garage."

The name meant nothing to me at the time. Later, it would all fall into place. I do not think Kid Rock realized how close I had come to giving him the beating of his life.

Whenever Huckaby or Billeebob were DJing at St. Andrews, I got a chance to warm up the crowd with my music. It took me a while, but I learned the ropes, and my skills improved.

This gave me enough exposure to start securing gigs of my own. I must have DJed at every location that was available in Detroit—from the Packard Plant, Timbo's, and under the Ambassador Bridge to Ann Arbor, Windsor, and Four Bears. The scene was still very small, and folks were still working to push the movement into mainstream society. I even threw a rave of my own called "Believe" in downtown Detroit and even flew a couple of my favorite DJs in from San Diego just to help give the city some West Coast house flavor. It was a huge success, and I had an amazing time with amazing people.

In any event, I got the opportunity to spin my vinyl records next to some of the best DJs of my time, before they were ever world renowned. With all of that partying, I had to eventually realize that it was not mixing well with my plans for continued education. Staying up all night to enjoy the club scene was one thing; a career was another.

I had to make a choice. So I chose school and Carmen. We dated more seriously now, and I got my paramedics license after taking the test the first time. A lot of guys have to take it a few times before they pass. Soon after that, I married Carmen. As homage to my days as a Detroit spin-master, Sneaky Pete was my best man.

CHAPTER 7

SETTLING DOWN TO WAR AGAIN

"I am tired and sick of war. Its glory is all moonshine. It is only those who have neither fired a shot nor heard the shrieks and groans of the wounded who cry aloud for blood, for vengeance, for desolation. War is hell."

WILLIAM TECUMSEH SHERMAN

When I fell for Carmen, it felt right. The two of us were married in October 1998, and we picked a suburb just outside of Detroit where we could live and raise a family. For the next five years I worked for an ever-growing list of private ambulance companies. Detroit EMS was one of them. I was on the road all the time, carried with sirens blazing from one emergency to the next, an action figure doomed to be present at people's most traumatizing moments.

During that time, I saw the inside of dozens of emergency rooms and the faces of thousands of intent medical staff going about their duties. I was hooked on the red line action of the calls, a willing junkie ready to shoot up on adrenaline when anyone needed me. It just did not matter who they were or what had happened—men, women, children, babies. If the situation called for someone to take action and react, I was the right person for the job.

Time after time I rode that high calm as they come, my nerves steady as a sniper's breathing. I was born to exist outside of the drama while everyone was swirling around inside it—a person apart, free to act appropriately in the eye of the storm as the men and women around me were destroyed by the sheer force of it all. I was born for war; I just did not know it yet.

My level of focus, even back then, was the skill that would take me places. One way or another, if a person was put in front of me, I would find a way to fix them or die trying. It was that last part that eventually caught up with me. *You can't save everyone, Gage*, I would tell myself. But somehow I still managed to feel the guilt.

We got a call one day to a house out in the suburbs. A child had gone into some sort of seizure. By the time we arrived, his skin was a pallid blue, and he was barely breathing. Just vaporous wisps of life remained, a defeated body rattling out its last moments. We loaded the kid into the ambulance as I told the mother we were doing everything we could, and we rushed him to the ER.

But he was gone by the time we arrived. The trick with seizures is to pump the patient full of valium, but you have to arrive in good time for it to work if they happen to react to it at all, in some cases such as this one. We were just too late that day. You cannot explain that to a grieving mother; you have to shoulder it yourself.

If you wanted to move up the chain from being a paramedic, a lot of guys would do their Firefighter 1 & 2 certificate. Of course, there was no guarantee that you were going to get a job. For every man with a qualification, there were at least 300 vying for the same job. I did not care. The Oakland fire had been enough to convince me that I could do well in that field.

I went to Firefighter School at Schoolcraft College and got my certificate in 1999. That was when I started applying for a position as a firefighter anywhere I could. I did a stack of written tests, had dozens of face-to-face interviews, and drove hell's acre damn near flat. Then, all of a sudden, I was offered three consecutive positions in three different towns.

My choices were Redford, Royal Oak, and Dearborn. I had just left Redford and did not want to go back, so I crossed that one off the list. Royal Oak would be a nightmare thanks to its legendary nightlife and party scene, and I had enjoyed enough shit from drunk people during my years as a bouncer. That left me with Dearborn.

It was March 2000 of the new millennium when I had my first day at the Dearborn Fire Department. I would fill a dual role as firefighter and paramedic for the team. Once again, I was exposed to a world in pain. Firefighters do not just deal with towering infernos; they deal with emergencies just like police do.

I saw domestic violence, sexual abuse, cars that had been torn in two by drivers so drunk that they could not stand up straight, kids thrown from crashed vehicles, suicides, and kids that had written their own suicide notes in wax crayons. Most of all, I saw a lot of people that were on a lot of drugs—rugs of all kinds, legal and not.

It seemed to me like everyone in Dearborn was taking too much of something just to make it through the day. I lost count of how many people I helped recover from overdoses.

I lost count, but I never stopped feeling all of that pain. The pain of living a life they did not expect. The pain of being cheated out of health, family, happiness, love, and money. So much pain.

Then the day came when I went to work and the world was set on fire. It was September 11, 2001. I had been in the kitchen with the boys shooting the breeze when the news story broke that morning. Surreal, gut-wrenching images straight from a Hollywood action movie. Only it was not action when it happened in real life. It was horror.

I had seen a hundred fires, but none burned into my memory like the flames coming off the towers on that TV screen. All of us were silenced. We felt the cold chill of a disaster creep in, the kind that settles on your chest like a frozen cat. I had a feeling deep inside me that this was the beginning of something. I already knew what part I would play in it.

The moment Carmen heard about the towers, she called begging me to come home. Everyone was scared in a way I had never felt before. Fear had always energized me to action, though, so when I could, I took off for home. It was best to be with family in times of national crisis.

The days ticked by, as did the months. Soon my wife became pregnant, and in May 2002 we had our baby daughter, Sophia Harmony. I was there when she was born and was the proudest father in the hospital that day. Some kinds of happiness linger, and a light was definitely struck in me on the day of Sophia's birth. Witnessing a miracle—check that off the list.

After a few more glorious years, I had landed myself in a tight spot with the City of Dearborn. While assigned to the ladder truck that week for being on cooking duty at Station

#4, we received a call at around 3 a.m. for a combative patient who might not be of sound mind (drugs). While assisting the two paramedics on the rescue with the patient, while still in a combative mode, he struck me twice in the face, damaging my right eye, breaking blood vessels, and causing nerve damage. I was in a complete daze and thought I was being attacked. Having the military training and skill set the City wanted to hire, I protected myself, not by hitting back but by securing his hands and arms to his chest as he lay on the stretcher inside the rescue.

Since I had knowledge of the two paramedics (male and female) in a secret relationship (he was married), this was the perfect opportunity for them. They wrote me up for attacking the patient and never assessed me of my injuries. Instead of keeping it in-house for the Station Captain to deal with, it went straight to the Fire Chief, who was brand new to the position, about three weeks at this time. He never said one word to me and just let the City try to fire me. The patient had no injuries; he was found to be on drugs that night, and no one even bothered to ask about my injuries and pain, including a completely blood-red sclera for a month. The union fully supported me and knew this was 100% wrong. I was suspended without pay during arbitration.

After a month of going back and forth between lawyers and also attending counseling, which I volunteered for, I decided that I was not going to put my life on the line for the rest of my career for a city and fire chief that did not want me. Once that is lost, it is just lost, so I resigned from Dearborn Fire. Why put my life on the line for a City that would not even back up their own firefighters? I could not respect them anymore, and I did not want their dirty paychecks either.

Suddenly, I found myself with a young family and no

source of income. I was desperate and dealing with the total injustice of it all. I made some calls to see what I could trump up. One of my buddies back from my old platoon at Camp Pendleton told me that things were happening out in Iraq. A war was about to kick off, and there was money in it for the right people that were willing to take on private work.

As luck would have it, I was the right kind of person. Recon Medics and alike always had a place with private security companies if we wanted it, he told me. Two calls later and a company called Blackwater had picked me up for work. The only snag would be the 9 to 12 months security clearance that needed to happen.

I did not even know if I was eligible yet, so while Blackwater was a long-term plan, I needed something for the short term. It was my responsibility to put food the table and care for my family, so I called another friend of mine, Chas. We had worked together as paramedics back in the day, and he was running the ER at Wyandotte Hospital as an RN now.

It was a good thing too because he managed to get me a paramedic position in the ER right away. I worked triage, pediatrics, Code Team, and HAZMAT for about a year until my security clearance finally came through. The State Department only had to issue my clearance, and I would be on the next plane to Iraq. A month before I was due to deploy with the Blackwater boys, Carmen and I were watching a special on *Dateline*[6] about security contractors in Iraq. We watched the video of four armed contractors, Scott Helvenston, Jerry Zovko, Wesley Batalona, and Mike Teague, who were killed and dragged from their vehicles. Their bodies were beaten and burned, with their charred corpses then dragged through the city streets before being hung over

---

6   https://en.wikipedia.org/wiki/2004_Fallujah_ambush

a bridge crossing the Euphrates River. She turned to me and insisted that I was not going anymore. I told her there was no turning back now; we needed the money.

After a heated debate, I finally agreed to try to find a position with another company, someone other than Blackwater. The State Department had granted contracts to two other companies for security work in Iraq, and I could try them both. So I called Triple Canopy and SOC the next morning to see what could be done.

That afternoon Triple Canopy had hired me. I told my wife that it was a completely different company, even though it did exactly the same thing. She still did not like the idea of me going, but at that point, my mind was already in Iraq. The only difference to me was that I would be helping soldiers instead of civilians. I loved that military feeling of brotherhood and connection and the ability to help support and protect our nation and our interests.

In September and October 2005 I went on a WPPS course with the DOS. With that completed, I was certified as a Worldwide Personal Protection and Security Specialist and was placed on a plane to Basra, Iraq. It was tough saying goodbye to my family, but I was excited to get back in the field. I had no idea what to expect when I arrived.

It was 105 degrees in the shade that day. The helicopter touched down on the airstrip lightly, like a dragonfly on still water. The sky was a piercing blue, and there was not a cloud in sight when I first stepped onto the tarmac with my gear. The first thing that struck me was the dry air; it was like inhaling a mixture of dust and heat. Throw in the aroma of some jet fuel and overflowing port-a-johns, and then call it home. The wind leapt at you, carrying with it the smells of war—hot, wet garbage, raw petroleum, human waste, and rotting flesh, in case you were wondering. I wondered if it was dead people or dead animals in the air. It took me several weeks before I could leave my hooch without openly gagging, and even then I had to fight back the overwhelming need to retch with the right gust of wind in the right direction. If smell was anything to go by, I was in for a tougher time than I had ever imagined. This was a different kind of war. The mood had been different from the Gulf War some years earlier. The previous war had not been fueled by so much anger and hate as there was now. Death hung in the air, stuck to your clothes, clung to your hair, and tainted your food. It was everywhere.

That first day we arrived at Basra Palace, a compound that we would use as our base of operations. I was picked up by our site manager at the helo-pad and dropped off in front of the embassy with my gear. Everyone was standing outside in front during a eulogy in honor of the four TC contractors[7] who were on mission and killed in an attack just a week prior. This was my hello to war. After it was over, I began going through my orientation and was told the rules of the Camp. Basra Palace was actually three palaces lined up in a row along the Shia River. The palace was imposing and grand, made of sand-colored stone just like everything in Iraq. One of the palaces had belonged to Saddam Hussein, and the other two were given to his sons. On a clear day like that, you could see far across the other side of the river and into neighboring Iran. The Americans, or "Yanks" as we were called, had converted the palace into a compound for use as an embassy during the war. The UN had also come along and set up facilities inside the base along with British military personnel and other various coalition members.

---

7   http://articles.latimes.com/2005/sep/08/world/fg-iraq8

At any one time there were some 700 people in the palace, with large quantities of equipment, vehicles, and logistics. The palace was always on the highest alert, the threat level at its greatest. As a result, it was not uncommon to see people striding around the palace with purpose, heading off to do some other important work for the war. There were always people coming and going, and missions were constantly on the go. It was a strange and mystical place, a palace that had been converted into the epicenter of war.

Triple Canopy, the company that I had signed on with, ran security for all U.S. Embassy and State Department personnel. Whenever someone important decided to leave the shelter of the palace and exit the gates, we would be charged with their protection. Easy enough. On arrival, we were led to these long rows of trailer-style housing, stacked like dominoes within the encampment.

If you can imagine a trailer park with a serious land shortage, that is what we had to deal with. Narrow, snaking passages passed through prefab buildings, where the temporary housing would house temporary base members. If you stayed long enough, you got to know the names of each of these pathways, and they became our palace alleyways.

A "hooch" is what we used to call these trailers, and they were almost worse than camping in many respects. Each hooch had the same identical layout: two cramped bedrooms, one on either end, with a common bathroom located in the very middle. You would have to share your hooch with another contractor until you had been there for more than a year.

Then, perhaps, if you had earned it, you could have a shot at your own private digs. And this was only if one was available. With the constant movement throughout the palace and new troops arriving all the time, you had to act fast.

The quality of life was poor, and the living was always rough in those cramped trailers. If you happened to be a medic like I was, you could say goodbye to the "extra" few feet of space you were given in your room. It was taken up by your gear and supplies. So I slept there that first night, trying to acclimatize to the claustrophobia and lack of air. I never did.

Fortunately, I arrived in Iraq just as the Mahdi militia were reaching their peak. Each day they would hit us hard with mortar attacks, chipping away at the security walls around the compound. These walls were always under small arms fire of some kind, usually RPG. Strategic points were regularly hit in the hope that the insurgents could find a weak spot and spill into the compound.

When mortars rained down, all personnel inside the compound were put on lockdown until the bomb dogs had done a sweep for unexploded ordinance. It happened every week to the point of every day. I heard incoming mortars launched so many times that I learned how to tell by the sound how far away the launch position was and when the shell would hit, so I knew about how much time I had to react.

I had to dash from the bathroom so many times that I learned to wash myself quickly in three minutes flat, no lingering. We would retreat to the bunker, where it was safe, and killed a lot of hours down there. In the Triple Canopy compound, we maintained three separate high threat security mobile escort teams.

Each was made up of at least a four-car motorcade package. There would be a vehicle for our principals, one lead vehicle, a follow vehicle, and a quick reaction force vehicle that also acted as the scout vehicle sometimes. Depending on how many principals we would have to protect, the size of the package went up from there. How important they were and where they wanted to go also mattered.

As the team medic, I was assigned to the main principal in one way or another, either by riding with him or in the follow vehicle directly behind as a shooter. I had two jobs, and both were just as important as the other. I was always a shooter first as security, and safety was our main objective, but when the shit hits the fan, then it is time to decide when to stop shooting and when to start patching holes. For obvious reasons, my role was to always be next to the main honcho, shielding him from danger. If something cropped up, I was his one-man security force and tactical combat casualty care medic.

In the vehicle the mobile security force, I kept a constant 360 degree watch on all terrain that we passed. The rear seats were modified so that you could face out towards the right side window and the left one too. Every man travelled with maximum gear load. We had our standard issue M-4s and Glock 19s, but the boys in the back would bring along 240 and M249 SAW machine guns, both belt fed with ten cans or more of ammo.

The huge black GMC Suburbans were armored and could stop small arms fire, but if a PKM or higher decided to attack our motorcade, we would be little more than flaming residue after target practice. Well aware of these flaws, each private contractor used their eyes to survey the threatening landscape so that evasive maneuvers could be taken should one pop up.

The fact was those Suburbans were so damn heavy that we were afraid that they would flip over from the rough ground, stranding us somewhere. With the risk of being flipped, shot at, blown to high hell with an IED or RPG or attack by heavy fire, our nerves were on edge. Every single man on the motorcade team had a huge responsibility. In a combat environment, there are no margins for error. Even little mistakes can cost you dearly out in the field.

In combat you are only as good as the man next to you, and out there, you had to rely on each other. If the mistake was big enough, lives would be erased, and no one wanted to be responsible for that. Having each other's six was second nature to all of us. If one guy was having a bad day and screwed up risking our security, the man next to him would compensate. That was a major part of the job description.

I knew someone always had my back because I had theirs. No matter how messed up a situation became, you knew you could trust in your team. It was impossible to be out there in a foreign, hostile territory without anyone looking out for you. That was how you get shot. A day came that year when the weather turned from hot into scorching as the summer months steamed us from the inside out. Our team was in the middle of routine training at the Palace Embassy compound when a huge explosion echoed through the barracks. It was much, much louder than usual. Immediately, I knew it was not a mortar. Judging by the sound, it was not that far off. Judging by the directional volume, something had been hit in the sky.

We looked up and could see a cloud of smoke over the rooftops of Basra. Unclipping our radios, we listened in to the chatter to hear what was going on. Nobody seemed to know exactly what was struck, although there were many theories. My team and I jumped into our vehicles and raced over to our TOC (Tactical Operations Command).

When we got there, word was spreading that a helicopter had been shot down over the city. No one knew for sure what it was or who was in it. But at that point in time, it did not matter; time was of the essence. American or not, it was our job to lend support to all combat teams. Several of us leapt into separate Bearcat vehicles, which were heavier and more protected than the Suburban vehicles, and we made for the gate.

Our company had received them for use in security and medical transport not long before this incident happened. We definitely felt a lot safer in them. The added gun turret and space for a few extra shooters made them tactically stronger. As my team approached the compound gate, we merged with a convoy of British soldiers that had also geared up.

The second we rolled out we were mobbed by a large number of people. The situation turned ugly almost instantly. Looking through my Bearcat porthole in the back, it seemed as though there were thousands of angry, shouting Iraqis surrounding us. As we neared the crash site, the smoke grew thicker and closer to the ground.

The helicopter had smashed into a house and was hanging over a rooftop engulfed in flames and power lines that were broken and sparking madly from the wreckage impact. The Bearcat slowed as rocks and other heavy objects began to ping off the armor. People were throwing things at the vehicle, and the situation was fast becoming violent.

Inch by inch we crept forward, the rocks getting bigger all the while. The people were chanting, uniting against us. Everyone in that vehicle knew that these people were related to the militia that bombed us regularly. Then we started to see Mahdi soldiers out on the street with guns. A Molotov cocktail exploded on the armor outside then another and one more.

The soldier who had been perched in the gun turret was forced to drop down and latch the lid when a rock hit him in the head. The closer we got to the crash, the thicker the crowd became. We were in danger of knocking people over or, worse, having to engage in a full-blown street fire fight.

Word came over the wires that the helicopter was British and that there were no survivors. Their own boys were given the task of recovering the bodies, so there was nothing to do but turn around and head back. As we turned, we spotted the chopper with two men inside it still on fire. Even if they had survived the crash, the crowd would have killed them.

The British troops had already hit the ground and were trying to take control of the situation. We needed to get out of there before things escalated. We heard shots ring out, and more people joined the crowd from the surrounding buildings. As we turned around, we spotted an RPG tube in the crowd.

People were climbing all over the Bearcat, trying to flip it over by then. Our driver was screaming at the people outside. Our team was getting more nervous by the second. There were calls to open the doors and waste some people to protect ourselves. We were lucky it never came to that. Our driver broke free, and we sped back to the Palace Embassy.

After the incident report, we tended to our vehicles. The damage was not too bad, with only a few window cracks and some bullet indents. The crowd had lethal intent, that was for sure. Back in my room, I stripped down and took a hasty shower. I was leaving for home in less than a week, and I was glad to be alive.

CHAPTER 8

SURROUNDED BY THE ENEMY

"The time to take counsel of your fears is before you make an important battle decision. That's the time to listen to every fear you can imagine! When you have collected all the facts and fears and made your decision, turn off all your fears and go ahead!"

GEORGE S. PATTON

Tensions on the street in Basra were rising. Soon after our first encounter, and just days before I was due to be sent home, we were sent out on a meet and greet mission. The call came down that we would have to ferry a handful of State Department big shots and VIPs to a secret location where talks would happen.

We were told in advance that we would have to head to three separate locations. The principals would be conducting business with the local Iraqi government officials. We did not know what they would be talking about, but from what we could gather, the conversation centered around old projects, new projects, and money.

The meeting was quiet enough, although that dreaded feeling of unease follows you like a shadow when you are outside of the compound. They offered us some traditional tea, and humor lightened the mood. In the end, everyone walked away happy. Before we set out for the next scheduled meeting, we geared up our five-vehicle motorcade.

First, the usual QRF team, which was also acting as an advance vehicle, left to scout ahead of us then set up somewhere in hiding. They would warn of any incoming trouble or contention from the urban residents. The mission was set to last four hours, and with this knowledge, we prepped for action and mentally stilled ourselves. The reality of war is that when you go out on a mission, there is no guarantee you will make it back.

Because of this sobering fact, it was tradition to get a few laughs before we piled in and set off. These laughs were always at someone else's expense. The more missions you ran and the longer you stayed in a war-torn area, the better you became at deflecting your feelings this way. Numbing your negative thoughts and fears is an important process of survival.

The mood needed to be light and breezy, so you had to check your baggage at the gate. Dragging that along with you was a great way to catch a bullet. If the guy on your left was going through the nastiest divorce you had ever heard about and he was dwelling on it constantly, then his head would not be in the mission.

The only thing more dangerous than being unfocused in battle is being ill equipped. The guys would mess with each other to keep their minds in the present. If it seemed like someone was drifting, you had to pull their heads back into it or risk disaster. This took a bit of time to learn due to such a diverse team of highly trained and skilled Type-A personalities. A team is only as strong as the links that bind it, and an unfocused mind is a broken link in that chain.

I was the team medic, so I had to make sure everyone's head was on straight. Evaluating the mental health of my team was one of my most important duties. If I felt a soldier was not hacking it anymore, I had to report him as a liability to our team safety. That was my job: to be the asshole who teased and to be the asshole who reported on them.

I remember a teammate in Iraq while working with Triple Canopy. He was above the average IQ and seemed to have no fear, and I respected him; his call sign was "Rainman." After a few years, he made it up to Team Leader, and I was his medic for a bit. During a mission, I felt he made a very poor decision, against everyone else's opinion in the vehicle, and put everyone at a dangerously high risk. I felt it needed to be addressed and spoke with him about it, but he stood his ground on what he did. In my opinion at that time and under those conditions in a war zone, this needed to be taken up the chain of command. I reported it to our senior Team Lead, "Beefy," and he then spoke with Rainman.

A couple hours later Rainman came almost barging into my room, yelling at me about what I did. I stood my ground and tried to explain why I reported it, but he would not hear it. I ended up going to another team to keep us apart since he hated me at that point and continued to be a Team Lead.

But my team respected me for it. It was a necessary function to keep the team alive. During my career overseas, I was only forced to do this on two separate occasions, both times in bloody Iraq. There was a third time, but it went unreported because I was to blame. We were 20 miles out of the gate when it dawned on me that I had left the medic gear behind.

A lot happened in 2007, and things had started to go south with my wife, Carmen. We had argued over Skype and Instant Messenger for the last four or five days, and my head was a wreck. While preparing my gear for our vehicle, my thoughts had been on my home life, on screwing up my relationship with Carmen, and on my daughter back home.

I missed my daughter, and my wife was not the woman I left behind two years before that. Just as we were reaching our destination, I pulled my head back together, and my heart nearly exploded. I realized with electric jolts rippling through me that I had left the medical gear back where we had staged our vehicles.

I had no advanced airway gear if we got hit, no serious blood stopping supplies or blood volume expansion logistics. I had royally, unforgivably fucked up. All we had were the small one-man basic medic kit that we each carried on our person. Our entire rolling medical unit was just standing outside in the sun, cooking in the summer heat.

I was beyond lucky that nothing happened on that mission. When we got back, my medic kit was not there. I looked all over the place, but I could not find it. The only thing to do was to retreat to my room, drop my kit off, and write an incident report, turning myself in. How was I going to explain losing two entire medical supply bags? I was in trouble.

When I arrived at my hooch, there was a hastily-scrawled note tacked to the door. "Head over to KY's room." KY was the driver of the vehicle that had been directly in front of ours during the mission. I headed there immediately and rapped on the door.

"Come in" came KY's voice. As the door swung open, there were my two medic bags perched on the floor.

I was relieved and angry at the same time. "What the fuck, KY. Where did you find them?"

He was going through his magazine pouch on his bed. "We doubled back to grab an extra radio at the TOC, and I saw them sitting there on the ground," he said casually.

"Why didn't you radio back and tell me? I've been freaking out!" I said to him, my temper rising.

"Shit, by the time I threw them into the back of our Suburban, our VC was screaming at us over the radio to catch up in a hurry. You know how crazy that man gets. I forgot all about it until we got back inside the gate just now," he said, pausing to speak.

"What if we had gotten hit?" I insisted.

"I would have told you."

"And what if you got hit first?"

"Good thing I didn't."

I felt sick to my stomach, like a thousand eels were reeling around in my intestines and trying to get out. I learned a very valuable lesson that day. From then on, I took my responsibilities a lot more seriously than I had before. If I fucked up, my entire team could easily die. On the day of the DOS mission, we sifted through our normal pre-mission preps.

After a pre-mission brief, a mission brief, a vehicle communications check, and a battery of personnel communication checks, we were ready to head out. Being able to fight against worst case scenarios was our duty. We anticipated the worst and left nothing to chance. Our lead vehicle had our team leader in it, with two Suburbans in the middle where our principals sat and the follow vehicle where I had been placed.

I faced a window, like the other security shooters, a job

reserved for Window Lickers, who had to survey and respond if necessary. If a tire blew, I would be half of the two-man team elected to get out and repair it. The QRF scouting vehicle left 20 minutes before our five-car motorcade rolled out of the gate.

Everyone was in full banter, their early mission humor sharp and healthy that day. The jokes were light and amusing, and I could see that all of us were laser focused. The first stop was a right side drop off where we would have to escort the package to the desired location. The DOS personnel met up with the locals and shook hands then settled down to talk money.

As the medic, I had to shadow the main principal, so I got to hear a lot of scheming and negotiations. We enjoyed tea and snacks, although I have to say the Afghan variety later on appealed more to my taste. The eats were something special, dates picked right off the trees. I still do not remember tasting anything that good in my life.

The next leg of our mission took us through Nasariya, a very busy city in Iraq with a large population of people. At 11h00 hours, we passed through the center of the town, a familiar site that we were used to from previous missions. Our vehicles were staggered in increments with enough space between them to fit another four or five cars in 25- to 30-meter stretches.

Our vehicle kept swerving left then right, so the road that we were on was not as straight as it could have been. As a Window Licker, I watched the city streak by, running through a continuous 360 security sweep. City areas exposed us to more danger, and attacks there made us a lot more vulnerable than out in the sticks somewhere.

My instincts had become very sharp thanks to the constant

threat level, and I was always on the alert for any signs of danger in peak form. At that stage, being on high alert was a natural state for us, a requirement of urban survival in Iraq. We could not turn it off if we wanted to. No one was talking anymore, and silence gave way to sounds around the city.

No one in the motorcade wanted to get stuck in a city, especially not in Nasariya. The place was famous for sudden small arms fire, RPG attacks, IEDs, and sticky bombs. If you were not careful, children would ride up to your vehicle on a bicycle and attach a bomb, which would stick magnetically to the surface. Then everyone inside would die.

Often the most innocent-looking people were the most suspicious; at least that is what we came to learn in this godforsaken place. The moment you stopped the vehicle, you became an even bigger target. Our vehicles may have been armored, but they were nothing like military vehicles and very vulnerable to bombs and skirmishes.

I was still staring out of my window conducting surveillance when the driver and VC yelled at the same time, in dual panic. "Watch the fuck out!" I spun around to catch what had happened at the front of the vehicle. A teenage boy had darted across the street in front us, and we narrowly missed him. It must have been a second later when his little brother did the same.

It all happened very quickly. We had just dodged the brother when a younger child, not looking where he was going, followed in tow. It was a millionth of a second, a yell rang out and the brakes locked and screeched in protest, but it was too late. I watched the little boy's head turn towards us just as the front grill collided with his body.

I was thrown forward, almost entirely into the front seat, and a body ahead of us was thrown up into the sky. I will never forget that moment. Our vehicle skidded on gravel and stopped in a sudden cloud of dust and debris. I looked up and saw the boy lying motionless on the road.

"Get up," I said aloud, wishing that the boy was all right. We all sat there frozen, in shock. Our driver was staring straight at the little boy's body, his hands white knuckled on the steering wheel. He was waiting for a command from the VC. We were the last vehicle in the motorcade, and everyone else had already moved on.

All alone in Nasiriya, stationary in an ill-prepared vehicle after just running over a child, it was one of those worst case scenarios we had never planned for. A crowd of people were gathering around the boy and around our vehicle. People seemed to flock to the area in moments, like they knew what was coming.

There were so many people that we could not start the Suburban back up or someone else would be hit. Chaos was surely brewing, and we were in the center of it. Our VC got on the radio and called in the news to our team leader. They called back to say that they were now canceling. The main mission was the safety of the package.

Because of this, the best course of action was to get back to the Tallil base in double quick time. Once the principals were safe, they would send backup. Until then, we were alone. My mind flicked through 1,000 different scenarios like an old movie projector. I made a decision, grabbed my medic bag, and reached for the vehicle door. "What the fuck are you doing, Gage?" said the Window Licker on my left. The VC turned and stared at me with horror etched into his face.

"You are not going out there," he said firmly.

"Then tell me what to do. Right now all I see is a fucked up kid that we hit and a bunch of pissed off people that think we don't give a shit," I said in return.

"The last thing we need is American contractors killing kids," said the VC almost to himself.

"Maybe we already have. The least I can do is go out there and see how bad he is." Again the VC told me to stand down. Before we made a move, we needed an interpreter. He called ahead to the TL in the first vehicle and gave him a brief report of the situation.

"How soon can you get the interpreter back here?" I listened as the TL explained that they would meet up with the QRF vehicle, transfer the interpreter to them, and have them return to us as soon as possible. You could not blame them; they were just following protocol. In a situation like this, though, crowds can turn violent in an instant. We had no time.

The crowd continued to expand, breathing in fury and exhaling hate as if it was a single living organism. I kept searching the road ahead of us for the hurt child, wondering how bad he was and hoping that he would move, sit up, stand, or something. The crowd thickened, and I lost all sight of him. I could feel the sentiment of the people outside.

Something moved in me, and I cracked the door. The VC yelled at me again, "You are to wait until the interpreter gets here and backup arrives!" He did not understand. He was making the wrong call.

"Goddamn it!" I shouted. "If we just sit here and wait for the kid to die, they are going to turn on us."

"And what if he is already dead?" demanded the VC. "You'll be walking into your own suicide."

I paused for a moment and took a sharp breath. "Fuck it. We have to look like we care." I grabbed both med bags and swung open the door. "I'm leaving my M-4 here. The more I look like a medic, the less of a threat I'll be." I knew that a gun would do me no good in a crowd this size. If they wanted me dead, I would be killed gun or no gun.

The second I jumped from the vehicle, the crowd closed in around me. They started yelling at me from all directions, outraged by what had happened. My VC and the other contractors jumped out to cover me, but they kept their weapons low in case the threat inflamed the crowd. Since most people knew what a stethoscope around the neck meant, I put mine on and held my medic bag up high enough so the medic symbol placed on the front of it could be seen.

I waded through the crowd saying, "doctor," several times as angry face after angry face pressed in on me. The stethoscope trick worked, and most people got out of my way. I made it to the boy without too much trouble. My heart sank as I reached him; he had not moved a muscle since I had seen him from the car. No one offered care of any kind or had tried to help him. They all just stood around staring.

It was clear that they cared more about an excuse to incite violence with us than they did about the boy. It made me even more nervous, and my breath caught in my throat. I had another concern to deal with—was the kid booby trapped? He could have been loaded up before he dashed out onto the street, or someone in the crowd could have placed a bomb on him before I arrived. Anything was possible in Nasariya.

I checked to see if any device was attached to the kid as best I could, torn between helping him and saving my own ass. I dropped my bags and knelt at his side. There was blood under most of his body, and his right leg was bent in the wrong direction, definitely broken. His eyes were wide and staring.

People began to shout at me, shunting each other around

and pointing at the boy. They blamed us; they blamed me. The boy was dead. When the VC asked me for an update, I replied with a vague response in case anyone spoke English. "He's gonna miss dinner." I used my hands to sweep under his body, checking for injuries and hidden bombs. The back of his head was completely split open, and I felt brain matter in his hair. At least he died instantly, no pain at all. There I was in a crowd full of hostiles with a child we had just accidentally killed. As long as they thought the kid could be helped, they had good reason to leave me alone. The instant they realized he was dead, they would surely kill me.

Having worked on countless people with traumatic injuries, including open head wounds, my paramedic instincts kicked in. I had to keep working with this kid the best I could until help arrived.

As I began to sweep his lower body, the Iraqi police forced their way through the crowd in a pick-up truck and parked a short way off from where I was crouched.

I looked up to find a PKM pointed at my head. Suddenly the crowd had become much bigger and much louder. A few of the Iraqi police went to chat with my VC. I heard him put in an urgent call for the interpreter. The situation was getting desperate, and hostility was becoming palpable.

The TL made a quick decision, transported the interpreter to his vehicle, and called for the QRF vehicle to now change course and meet up with the two-car package still on its way back to Tallil base. No one would waste time, but no one had to die either. The crowd was yelling at the police, and they were yelling at us all in a language none of us understood.

Arabic was not an easy language to learn, so even though we had been there for years, I had no idea what was being said. Things were heating up, and the entire time, I just crouched down, over this dead kid, a gun to my head, pretending that he was alive. More pick-up trucks arrived on the scene. It was the Iraqi National Army heading towards me.

They pointed their weapons at me too. The people around me started to grab at my uniform and punch and kick at me. I focused on working on the kid. Everyone wanted us dead, and I was getting nowhere fast, frozen to a corpse I would soon be joining. I radioed through to my VC, "How much fucking longer?"

"They're close!" he said back immediately.

My VC tried to work the IP and IA at the same time, all without any language skills. The man was a superstar. Just when I thought things could not get any worse, I felt the hard cold end of a rifle pressed up against the back of my head. I prayed and kept working. I had to stay busy. The instant I stopped, they would shoot me.

A few long seconds later and a young man pushed through the crowd and knelt down on the other side of the boy. He did not say a word. His eyes lingered on me then flicked back to the boy and then back on me. I was busted. Instead of yelling at me, however, he scooped the boy up in his arms and vanished into the crowd.

I was stuck, kneeling on the ground, that same rifle pressing a tattoo into my head and neck. I did not know what to do. It would be fast; I knew that much. I waited for my last moment, but it never came. Suddenly the gun was gone. I stood up and turned around; the shooter had disappeared into the crowd.

There were still a lot of angry people and a lot more guns pointed at me; I had to get out of there. At that very second, our TL arrived on the scene with the interpreter in tow. They spoke to the IA colonel while I stood there passively, still in shock. After about 10 minutes, it was decided that nothing else could be done.

The IA, the IP, and my TL exchanged some information with each other, and I was allowed back into the vehicle. We rolled out shortly after that. Everyone in the vehicle was talking enthusiastically on the way back to the base but me. I went through the medic bags to check if anything had been stolen while I had been working on the dead boy.

I stared at the barren terrain as we passed it, my mind still in that crowd in Nasiriya. I did not want to talk. We arrived back at the base, I completed my incident report, and that was that. A couple days later I found out that the child had been taken to the city hospital, but they would not take him because he had been killed by Americans.

They tried another hospital but got the same treatment. The only option was an American military base, so they brought the child back to us at Tallil. I do not know what was done with the body, but in order to maintain good faith with the locals, the DOS paid the family $10,000 American for their loss. That was the customary amount.

To them, it was like receiving ten million, so they gladly accepted it. For me, it was just one more nightmare in one more war that did not make any sense.

CHAPTER 9

THIS IS THE WAR

"Once we have a war there is only one thing to do. It must be won. For defeat brings worse things than any that can ever happen in war."

ERNEST HEMINGWAY

★★★★

The thing about war is that it is never as clean or as easy as one side believes it will be. Ego is the enemy of progress, and we had brought it with us to Iraq. It was not long after I had arrived at the waterfront that the U.S. brain trust had stalled. They had been running the show, unable to admit to themselves that a fully-fledged uprising was gaining momentum.

There was no "mission accomplished" or "we will be greeted as liberators." Our leadership's arrogant swagger soon turned into a hard slice of reality. Just like Vietnam and the Korean War before it, we had blundered into war convinced that we would discover a society in desperate need of a red, white, and blue knight.

Eventually, even the stuffed shirts had to admit that the whole affair had become a political embarrassment. We were too deep in it now to withdraw. Our only path forward was to wade through the mess we had created.

As our teams pondered this unfortunate outcome, IEDs exploded daily like a symphonic arrangement outside the gates, RPGs would regularly whistle by—inches from our heads—and mortar rounds peppered the compound where we slept until the ground looked like sand after a hailstorm. The Iraqi people had chosen anger, and they were blowing themselves—and us—to hell.

The country was in a state of upheaval, and the collective outrage of millions was being aimed in our direction. We deserved it. While coated in this thick cloud of madness, the Sunnis bombed an important Shi'a shrine in Samarra, prompting a sharp escalation in sectarian violence that even the hardest among us had to adjust to.

Every marketplace had cars, and every car could contain the next bomb. The friendly grocer on the corner would tear off his jacket, revealing a bomb before converting himself and everyone around him into pink mist and chunks of death. Suicide bombings became the new reality of war. People were dying in the hundreds, all at once and all at the push of a button.

This was the kind of fear that no army could train out of you. We headed out into this mess on a regular mission one day, with the usual client on board in our four-car motorcade. Instantly, we were greeted by aggressive crowds baying for blood. It got so bad we drove balls out back to the base a few minutes later as the familiar rhythm of small arms fire urged us inside the gates.

The crowd that day had turned on us suddenly, protesting

our movements and expressing their discontent by viewing every Western vehicle as a target. We had to take a different route through the city on our second try, and even then our vehicles sang with deflected bullets, rocks, and other large objects hurled at us as we drove by.

As we turned the corner, we nearly collided with a couple of British Army LAVs that were also being targeted by the crowd. LAVs had some serious firepower; they were tank-like and raw with eight wheels and a whole lot of attitude. The Brits would usually patrol alongside their LAVs, but no one would chance a run along today with the crowds so riled up.

Our motorcade quickly became boxed in by the rioting masses and the imposing LAVs ahead of us. Small arms fire nailed bullet necklaces along the floor, on buildings, and on our vehicles. When we tried to turn around, we noticed a young man step out of the crowd carrying an RPG. He was behind the Brits and aiming straight for all of us.

The flash went off, and the RPG took off towards us. "Look out! RPG!" our guys screamed to the Brits. It was over in a second. The RPG had flown right over the top of the two LAVs and our motorcade. The Brits that had been standing exposed in their top hatch nearly died of fright as the RPG missed them by inches.

The man that had shot the missile was running down the street, the RPG tube still balanced on his shoulder. The Brits were in a better position to eliminate the threat, but they did nothing. Not a shot was fired! I nearly cracked my door to open fire, confused at their response to nearly being roasted alive by a militant.

Back in the nearly-safe confines of the palace, I confronted the Brits about letting the RPG shooter escape. It turned out, the British rules of engagement forbid it. If an enemy was retreating and not actively shooting at them, they were not allowed to engage. It made no sense to me. In my team, if someone tried to burn us alive, they would not live to do it again.

As the months rolled by, I degenerated mentally and struggled with the separation from my family. It weighed on my mind, causing an on-going ache in my chest. The war had been a golden opportunity to make a lot of money, fast. I could pay off my house and cars, put money away for Sophia's future, go back to college, and eventually become a respectable American family man. That was the plan.

Not to mention the excellent health insurance and 30 to 90 days of vacation every year! Before I had gone, I saw the war as my ticket to a happy, stable life. But there is nothing stable about war. The longer I stayed, the greater the unease became. Then it happened. The end of the life I was trying to build. Carmen and I were ready to divorce.

I was abroad, fighting for my country and for my family's future, doing the best I could to be the man my father never was, and it still was not enough. I ended up 6,000 miles away with a head full of questions and a messy divorce. It was a fresh kind of hell, not being able to get back home when my life had fallen apart.

At night, instead of the fear of war, I had a new fear: surviving it. Again and again I saw my wife and child crying themselves to sleep because I was not there. My wife, depressed and lonely, had been abandoned by her husband. Sophia was lacking the attention she needed during the most important developmental years of her life. I had left, and it was all they could feel now.

When I awoke each day, I considered going back to the States, but there was nothing left for me there. I had walked out on the Fire Department after my own team had betrayed me, and once that happens, you cannot undo it. Who knows what struggles I left them with, when I had hopped on a plane? The other 400 applicants would be easier to hire.

I thought about getting my job back as a road paramedic, but I hated the idea. That alone kept me from it; the patient's deserved better than that. I had never been a man who could move backwards with ease. So I remained at war. I watched as my marriage and my family fell apart. The money was so great that I thought I was making the right decision.

I took on the risk to get them the reward they deserved, and that was my sacrifice. Why could they not understand that? The economy in America was beginning to plummet, and I knew what waited for me if I went back. As time wore on and my family ties weakened, I began to question all of that logic. Maybe there were other reasons I left my family.

Hindsight is a hot poker. It is easy to look back now and see what a mistake it was. My world crumbled around me. That was when Brian, aka "Hershey," stepped into my life. He was a blonde-haired, blue-eyed stereotype with the physique of a model and the humble nature of a much less attractive man.

Hershey had the biggest heart, and despite what happened, he was always happy about something. As Special Forces and a former Army Ranger Sniper with combat experience in Afghanistan, we connected right away. The man was fast, deliberate, and strong with a type-A personality. Some days it was like he drank adrenalin because his switch was always on.

Brian was a poster boy for the military. I do not remember a day when he was not ready for anything, prepared to take on the world with his brothers in arms. With the last name of Reese, he went from being called Reese's Pieces to eventually acquiring the call sign Hershey, and he became known as the master of pranks. With an extreme mindset, there was nothing Hershey would not do to fuck with someone if they deserved it.

Soon after I became friends with Hershey, I knew the two of us would be all right. Like almost everyone else that was shipped in to fight, Hershey began as a window licker and became the guy to my left in the backseat of our vehicle. He was an especially talented radio coms guy, with a flair for rapid, under-pressure communication that made a difference, and his shooting skills were top-notch.

If anything went down on a mission, Hershey was fearless in his approach to it. He was always the first man on point and the first to head into the fray. As we grew closer, I found out that he was also a Michigan native from the Ann Arbor area. Hershey loved his family and spoke of them often, and he had the same feeling about his work as I did.

The man was never in a bad mood unless he ran into something he could not understand. Then he became extremely brisk and direct, a consequence of his "no-BS"' personality. Both of us were total gym rats, so we started hitting the gym together, and this eventually progressed to training, team mission, and chow time.

Hershey ate like a horse. The compound was small enough, so we would run into each other at the community bathroom. We ended up talking while we shaved and showered and hung out together in his room or mine. Brian constantly spoke about his next big trip when he would rotate home and which women he planned to bang.

As always, our conversation would turn to the war and whatever political vomit was being spewed all over the American population on television. When the IDFs came in, we would flee to the same bunker and do our reports together too. He and I became really tight back in those days. The right term, I believe, is "battle buddies."

It is human nature to seek comfort in another human being, and when the guy sitting next to you has been there for months at a time, a friendship is usually struck. It becomes easy to spill your thoughts and feelings to someone that knows what you are currently living through. Doing the same dangerous shit every day forces you to find this companionship.

It happened to me at the fire department and on board the Navy ship in the Persian Gulf too. You need someone that understands so that your emotions do not get the better of you. Having no one to hear you is a quick way to lose your mind in a war.

Brian had told me all about a guy name Chaz Crawford, who he had met during his days as an elite U.S. Army Airborne Ranger.

When Brian joined the Army, he went straight into the elite U.S. Army Airborne Rangers, where he met Chaz Crawford during in-processing. They both served in Bravo Company, 3rd Battalion, 75th Ranger Regiment, together for their entire time in. They were as close as brothers, and they had a lot of great times together. We have shared countless stories, and Chaz was in a lot of them. They were both deployed together in support of Operation Enduring Freedom in Afghanistan. After returning from Afghanistan and ending their military tour of duty, Chaz went home to Louisiana to raise his family and start college. He also took care of his sick sister, who lived with them also. Brian did not want to leave the brotherhood he fell in love with, and now that he was out, he decided to join the contracting world. Brian joined AEGIS right out of the military and went back to Iraq. Chaz and his family had a hard time paying the bills while he was going to school. Chaz asked Brian to put in a good word for him, so Brian worked to get Chaz hired into AEGIS also. After Chaz was hired, he was placed at a different location than Brian in Iraq, working site security. Since there was more money to be made working for DOS and a tougher job all together, Brian and Chaz both applied for Triple Canopy and also for their secret security clearance. It did not take too long for Brian to receive his clearance, and he was soon moving into our Living Area (LA) somewhere. Chaz continued to work with Aegis, waiting for his clearance to come through so he could walk on to TC as well.

After only a couple weeks working with TC, Brian got the news. While on duty, a suicide bomber tried to get inside the area Chaz was securing. Chaz pushed forward towards the bomber to keep him away from the compound and personnel. It went off, killing Chaz. Brian blamed himself for this, feeling as if he left him behind somehow even though he knew it was all Chaz's decision; he just could not find a way to forgive himself somehow.

"Two days prior to his death, Chaz was promoted to the position of Team Leader. He was the paragon of a professional soldier, whose life was taken while doing what he felt God had meant for him to do. He will be intensely missed by all who were fortunate enough to know him.[8]"

Hershey was nearly always the life of the party, but he was very serious about war and how much he hated it. He would speak about the pricks in Washington, the military top brass, and the terrorists like they were all his enemies. If he could find a solid reason to hate something, he did. All his joking and pranking was a mask for his uncontrollable anger.

---

8   http://katytimes.com/obituaries/article_2ca2887d-55cb-582f-9ffd-dea56f94e070.html

The local paper did a write up on Chaz back home. It said, "Former U.S. Army Ranger Chaz Benjamin Crawford, age 23, was killed in Northern Iraq on March 14, while working for a private security company hired by the U.S. Department of Defense, protecting top U.S. military officers and diplomats. Chaz was the paragon of a professional soldier, whose life was taken while doing what he felt God had meant him to do. He will be intensely missed by all who were fortunate enough to know him." The emotional scars from the incident sank much deeper than any superficial wounds. He blamed himself for Chaz's death, and somehow he could never find a way to forgive himself for it. Nothing was the same after that. Brian struggled with survivor's guilt and was haunted by the memories of the day he lost Chaz. When Brian first came to me to tell me the news, I felt I was in more shock than he was. He said it with a straight voice, like it was old news. He gave me all the details he knew and again was straight voiced and almost emotionless. At the time, I assumed he was okay. We all had stories like that, so it was often you would hear a tragedy like this. We were all numb, plain and simple.

Hershey had a huge tattoo inked on his right side to commemorate the event. He would often show me his scars from the attack, like he hated them. We sat together many times as he recounted their last days, their movements, and what happened to Chaz. He would tell me the story over and over again of how Chaz saved his fellow teammates, as if talking about it would help his heart heal.

As far as I knew, Brian was never briefed after the bombing. Nobody came around to offer him any support or to chat to him about losing a friend. Not a soul from AEGIS, or anyone else for that matter, talked with him. It was an unspoken rule that you were expected to take it and move on.

Since Brian was still new to the company, I asked if he could be placed with my team. It was not a difficult request, and our site manager was always open to suggestions. Hershey and I were placed together on a team in Basra. I helped him recover after the loss of Chaz, and he helped me through my divorce. Sanity was the only thing that mattered, and having a good friend on my team straightened me out.

Later that year in June, we heard that some gunmen on motorcycles had opened fire on four local employees from the U.S. Regional Embassy Office. These workers had returned fire and were forced to seek refuge in a nearby residence until a Quick Reaction Force team could evacuate them to safety.

That was the story being circulated anyway. It was not the truth of what happened. Soldiers talk. Soon the talk spread through the compound, and we found out what really happened that day. One of our interpreters and a man I had worked with frequently through the Embassy had been found out and targeted by the Sunnis.

As he and his family were trying to get out of the city, the Sunnis attacked, killing all of them. Him. His wife. His two kids. They were executed by these gunmen. For a long time, I wondered why the brass would deny the real story. Why spread false rumors about what had happened to this innocent man and his family?

Then a day came when I understood the need to limit this kind of information. Some months later, we were nearly killed by a sticky bomb. We were driving along with our principal in tow when two kids on a motorcycle pulled up next to our vehicle. We saw them and aimed. They saw our guns and tried to get away.

The streets were cluttered with traffic, which made their escape difficult. Hershey leaned out of the vehicle door, aiming for a clear, clean shot. Our team was trained to kill. Shoot first, shoot true, no warning shots required. The first bullet had to be a deadly one—anything less was a punishable offense in our team.

As Hershey aimed, Bam Bam (a sniper and one of the members of our team) could see that he was going to kill these kids. He acted impulsively and shot out their front tire instead. The motorcycle swerved, causing us to do the same. Hershey nearly fell out of the vehicle; there was such mayhem for that split second.

When we arrived back at the base, Bam Bam was severely reprimanded for his actions. Our site manager and the State Department Security Officer grilled him about his behavior. Luckily, he got off with a warning and was not sent home then and there. I spoke to Bam Bam later that day about what happened.

That is when he told me what really happened to the interpreter and his family. I stood there as he showed me pictures of the car with the bodies still inside it. It was carnage. When you were witness to shit like that, you could understand why another version of the story was needed. Such violence made triggers easier to pull, no matter where they were aiming.

Some months later, four British service personnel were killed when their boat was attacked. It was a Sunday on the Shatt Al-Arab waterway just north of the palace compound. Intel began to trail in that there would be similar attempts to infiltrate our compound from the river. As a result, our company set up an overwatch rotation from the top of the Embassy building.

Those river attacks never happened. But a few times while I was on duty, IDF mortar attacks landed inside the compound from that general direction. We would just stand there, on the balcony of Saddam's sprawling palace, and watch them hit the ground somewhere below us. If one sounded like it was coming our way, we would head for cover. Most of the time it was a humbling show to watch.

The day came when another helicopter was shot down in Basra, and we were deployed to the crash site. We regularly clashed with the public during incidents like these, returning under mortar attack to the palace compound. That day we arrived back to find several hooches completely destroyed.

On September 22, 2006, while we were just returning from a training mission, we began to take on another mortar attack. We quickly threw the vehicle in park and ran for cover in a bunker. We noticed there was smoke and fire coming from inside our living area. As soon as we felt it was clear, we ran towards the area to see what we could do. A hooch was hit directly from above, and when the mortar hit the ground below, the overpressure blew the trailer wide open. A DOS representative named Julio had been killed as he was taking an afternoon nap. As we made our way inside, Julio was still lying in his bed almost as if nothing had happened. With a direct hit from above, the overpressure had blown half of his head off. The rest of him was charred but mostly intact. The mortar attacks got so bad after that, on one hellish day we had to abandon Basra Palace while it was on fire. It was damaged beyond repair.

Half of the compound had been on fire at some point, and the other half had been blown to all hell. We packed what we could and relocated to Basra Air Station. In the months that followed, we rebuilt the U.S. Embassy and everything that went with it. Our U.S. Embassy security guard force was increased and trained on an ongoing basis.

Mortar attacks were still common at the new base but not as well aimed because it was so large. Some of them did connect with important structures and inflicted damage. I was at the base hospital one day, checking on one of my patients, when we took a direct hit. If I had not ducked behind my metal table, the shrapnel would have torn me to shreds.

My team and I spent a lot of time getting the new Embassy up and running. We also focused on training the Iraqi forces to be our allies. I had a lot of issues with the logistics on the medical side. In the meantime, we continued with our missions outside the gate. It was a busy time, the likes of which words could never fully illustrate.

By January of the next year, my divorce with Carmen was final. Brian was fired from TC a couple of months later due to his increasing anger issues. He pushed a TCN in the bathroom after several attempts to stop him from washing his feet in our sinks, but still not a clever move. He returned to school in Louisiana to fulfill a promise that he made to Chaz, his family, and his sister. He sent me a poem he had written for college once, and he was slotted as a guest at my second wedding.

I was married to Roseanna, my second wife, later that summer. Two weeks after the wedding, I was back in Iraq, at war again. Hershey and Roseanna spoke a few times on the phone, and they tried to meet while I was deployed for mutual support. But it never happened. Roseanna found a message on Brian's Myspace page a month later.

She called me immediately in Iraq. Brian had been waiting at his house for some friends to show up for a night on the town. They arrived and found him dead. After several complaints to a few friends that he wasn't having any luck with the VA, a friend of his gave him a few oxycodone for the pain from his war injuries. He had never taken it before and thought it was better than nothing. He soon had an allergic reaction to the stuff, he did have a history of several allergies to medications in the past and he was fully aware of this as part of his medical history. But I also know PTSD robs you of your logic and your self-awareness and crushes your confidence to a point where you can either become very desperate or almost catatonic. It was your average dose, according to the autopsy. After everything he had survived, he died a senseless death and died alone.

CHAPTER 10

THE WAR COMES WITH YOU

"Always remember, if you have been diagnosed with PTSD, it is not a sign of weakness; rather, it is proof of your strength, because you have survived!"

MICHEL TEMPLET

It was 2010 before I managed to leave for home, fresh from the incident with the child we had knocked over and killed some months before. I had been in Iraq for four years and three months, and it had changed me. I was a different Gage. When you see the kind of things that soldiers like Hershey, Chaz, and I saw, the war never seems to be over.

I arrived home alive but broken from all that had happened. Roseanna was my only comfort, and I am sad to say that she had to deal with a lot from me. Post-Traumatic Stress Disorder sets you up to fail. It gives you a short fuse and an explosive response as you are forced to relive the trauma you once experienced.

Imagine a volcano triggered by the slightest tremors. That was me when I got back. Desperate to make a success of my life at home, Roseanna and I decided to start our own company. I had some investment money from the tour I had just completed, and I was ready to settle into a life of productivity, safety, and family.

As it was turning from lean to mean, I found myself panicked by my failed investment. No one could have predicted that my business model would instantly be nullified by this latest political development. I was crushed. Money became scarce, and I started to doubt my ability to keep the company going.

Instead of fighting to make my business succeed, I allowed the fear of financial loss to creep in and took on a number of part-time jobs. I lost so much usable time doing those badly paid jobs and was so busy frantically working for money that I lost sight of logic. Fear was driving me instead of my goals, and I lost my way. The business failed.

I sold off what I could to recoup some investment, all the while stressed out of my mind because I knew that my PTSD did not make me a great hiring prospect. Some days it felt like everything I had seen back in Iraq was shackled to my ankles. I dragged it all around with me, and it gave me a heavy gait. The PTSD threatened to take my sanity, my marriage, and my life more than once. I had good days and bad. There were days when I would be grateful to be home and days when I could not understand why I had ever left the war. It raged inside me, my thoughts clattering down like mortars in the palace compound. Eventually, it cost me my second marriage too.

Back then, cannabis was the only thing keeping me alive. Roseanna had introduced me to old acquaintance of hers in the summer of 2008, a man named Robbie. With the newly legalized medical position of cannabis in Michigan, a host of business opportunities became available for anyone willing to be a high risk first responder.

Robbie and his cousins used to run the city, selling drugs and getting into trouble as punk teenagers back in high school. A short, stubby man of 5'2", what Robbie lacked in looks he made up for in experience. I remember Roseanna told me he had been pretty into meth at one point, which made him compulsively fidgety.

With Robbie fresh out of jail, I found myself at a BBQ with this ex-con and my wife at the time. As they chatted and caught up, I grilled the burgers. Naturally, the cannabis reform in Michigan was a hot topic of conversation. I heard how Robbie's brother Darren had been growing for a long time and was doing very well financially under the new laws.

Darren lived about 10 minutes away from us in town. I admit, I was impressed by the figures that Robbie was throwing out. I asked Robbie if he would mind asking Darren to help Roseanna and me with an MMJ grow of our own. After so many years in Iraq, I was desperate to find something that could support us financially.

I would be home soon permanently, and I wanted to explore the idea. I had missed too many of Sophia's big moments and was running out of excuses. Watching your child grow up on Skype is a painful experience. I cannot even imagine how hard it must have been for soldiers in previous wars when all they had was letters or even nothing.

It all sounded wonderful, growing cannabis—the thing that had been helping my PTSD—for money. A perfect fit. I should have known it was too good to be true. That week I called Darren on the phone, and he answered my questions. I was told to read Jorge Cervantes' book, *The Marijuana Bible*, which I did, twice in three days.

I was fascinated by it all. Growing medical marijuana is a complex and intricate process. I found myself immersed in the history and knowledge of a plant so unique in nature that I found myself becoming converted 100%. I gutted one of our bedrooms and changed it into a grow room, where I established 72 plants. That was enough to help six medical marijuana patients legally.

I fell headfirst in love with growing cannabis. As an organic medicine, it was flawless, and better still, there were amazing financial possibilities. When I returned to Iraq that year, Roseanna continued to grow. But after three indoor attempts, the business was a bust. We drifted apart, gave up, and sold off the equipment.

I believed that it had been the end of my cannabis aspirations. While I continued to smoke certain strains, I stopped growing it. All the while, a nagging feeling ebbed in my stomach. Cannabis was soothing for PTSD. Up to that point, it had not cured it yet—no, but it had stopped much of the violence inside. It was an active barrier between me and oblivion.

When the businesses had failed, Roseanna had jumped ship. I became too despondent, beaten down, and difficult to handle because of the defeats that we sustained. It was not fair to her, and I do not blame her for leaving me. I was a deeply troubled man. But through it all, I discovered an enduring interest and love for growing, something that appealed to my chemistry and science background that gave me a sense of peace.

Once again I found myself lacking in the real world, and the magnetism of war called out to me. There, the violence made sense because it was on the outside. At home, the turbulence happened in your head, spilling out of you like a leaking memory tap. It did not take me long to start trawling the Internet for work overseas.

I immediately found a job with a British company working out of the Helmund Province in Afghanistan. Their regular medic had become ill and had to go home for a while, so they needed a temporary replacement. The pay was solid; I had more than enough experience in combat situations, and I had the right security clearance.

In the contracting world, it can be tough to find a decent all-round tactical medic with security clearance and WPPS training. For many companies, finding me was like striking gold! Only eight months had gone by since I had returned home to start my business and try again. I really worked my ass off at every angle I could to stay solvent.

I went to school, ran my (Mobil Production Medics) MMP business, and grew cannabis in the basement of my house. School was never a guarantee of income, so that was a bust. My paramedical staffing company for the TV and film industry in Michigan was a badly timed fiasco for us financially (thanks, Governor), and mold continued to destroy our medical crops with every grow.

Every odd job I took on made things worse for us. I sold off as much of the medical equipment as I could and resold the ambulance I had just purchased at a major loss. With these struggles cresting on me like a tidal wave, that "gold" status that I held with excellent paying companies abroad constantly played on my mind.

One miserable afternoon we found ourselves in front of a nice-looking pawn shop just off Ford Road in Canton. It was our best and only option at this point. I opened up my car door to go inside, but Roseanna did not budge. We were going to do this together; that is what we decided. But when I looked back and saw her face as she just sat in the car motionless, I knew words were not necessary. I already had it in my pocket, so I just closed my car door and went inside. About 45 minutes later, I returned to the car and to Roseanna, who had a fresh touch-up of mascara and a slight smile. I was fortunate to exchange the $14k ring I had worked so hard on with my buddy Cherry from TC (His dad was the jeweler) for $3,500 and a 15% off coupon for the pawn shop. She kept her dignity insatiably intact as her eyes held a cold pool of drowning memories. A scar like that will never heal.

I had to go back to war. The British company I reached out to was quick to respond. They had me on a plane to South Afghanistan, winging my way to the Helmund Province just outside of Nad-e-Ali. I would be there for a month. The job was to work high threat security for USAID personnel that were in charge of building a large Afghan National Army Base (ANA Base).

The sheer expanse of poppy fields there caused the Taliban to push hard for control, so there was an ongoing takeover plan that we had to short circuit. The landscape was sweltering and dry, and the American forces identified the need for a stronger base in the region so that control could be wrestled back and held.

The main problem was building that doggone base. The plans said that the base should be around the size of six football fields, so when I arrived, the skeletal beginnings had already been set. Four giant walls were being constructed to protect the buildings inside. We had a tiny compound nestled in the corner of this ANA base, little more than a couple of hooches on wheels.

These trailers were cramped, and they were built to be shared with another contractor. Inside, you could fit two single beds, two curio cabinets, and a small desk. In the middle of the trailer was enough room for a tiny bathroom, to be shared between four soldiers. It was like living in a jail cell; it was less cramped than a tent but more depressing to sleep in.

A guard tower was fixed into the walls around us, the gates had large locks on them, and we had our own bomb dogs, but the security was in a desperate state. The guys knew it was mostly for show. Our walls, after all, had some person-sized cracks in them. The building company that erected the walls did so poorly, from cheap materials.

There were only three to five USAID personnel in charge of the onsite project at any one time. I assumed several roles in this position as the site medic for all company and client personnel. To build the site in their chosen location, deals had to be struck. One of them was that only local nationals could work on the site.

No third party Ugandans, Kenyans, or Peruvians were allowed, even though they were the norm. In my experience hiring people from the same place where the war is going on is a bad idea. There are too many opportunities for sabotage and danger. They purposefully build badly, and over time, the guys sending the mortars into the compound got very accurate.

This is thanks to Intel being leaked out by the local builders allowed on site. It is exactly what happened in Basra, and it would happen here too. Getting these "impartial" locals to work on government installations and military bases is ignorant and causes a lot of problems. I often wondered how many local nationals worked in the Embassy in Benghazi before it was blown to smithereens.

Anyway, the British company that I worked for did not seem to mind. They received an amazing amount of money for every man on the ground, so the threat level was secondary. After one solid week's worth of hard travel, I arrived to a compound on high alert. It was Iraq all over again, only worse. Our defenses were pathetic, and we were outnumbered 10 to 1.

Dotted around the crumbly walls were 75 to 85 guards and about seven to eight contractors like me. Whenever a client needed to go outside the compound, I would work security detail. I also acted as vehicle commander of our second motorcade vehicle and as team medic. I trained the guards how to shoot their AK-47s with accuracy and taught them other necessary war time tactics, like how to kill quickly and how to avoid being killed in the process.

I hated it at the compound. Every day I resented the decisions that brought me back to this hell hole. The team would watch the front gate compulsively, assessing workers, guards, and our logistic support. The VIPs and contractors that moved through the base had to drive to a nearby British Army camp, where they could board a helicopter to Kandahar.

One week in, and the news was dire. The locals were furious at our presence, and political backing from nearby villages all the way to Lashkar Gah ensured that we would be attacked just as soon as the enemy training was complete. They practiced maneuvers often. Our best plan was to monitor the front gate and flee to the British Camp if things went south.

Added to this ever-worsening sequence of events was the fact that we had a shortage of weapons for the guards; only half of them were equipped. Passing weapons on to different guard shifts was a great way to ensure that the guns never fired clean bullets or functioned as intended. We took pot shots at the walls to keep the guards on their toes at night.

If an attack happened, though, there would be nothing we could do. The guards without guns, sleeping in their tents, were defenseless. Most guards were untrained, and the language barrier was more like a pair of earmuffs. Whenever I looked at them, all I could think about was who would shoot at us first when the time came.

Better to kill eight guys than die defending them. Over the years, you learn to analyze people and what their true intentions are. What they say and how they act can be false. You have to be aware that out there in the sand, even the guards you are training may be waiting for a moment to shoot you in your back.

With my training, I had developed a keen eye for security threats and safety issues, especially if they are imminent. Many contractors like me that have worked in war-torn areas develop this sixth sense. It is a necessary skill to possess to survive the place. You always had to be alert and on edge, cool and calm on the outside, with an aggressive attitude. If you were seen as a target at any time, you would become one. My roommates were Yugoslavian and Croatian, the friendliest guys you would ever meet. By the time the third week rolled around, we were hearing gunfire throughout the day. It came from all directions, along with five to seven mortars for good measure.

Sometimes they would aim at us, and sometimes they aimed at the British compound a short way away. One evening Darren and I were escorting a USAID client on a mission outside the compound when a British convoy trundled by. They often stopped inside our camp to take a break and chat. We had very little food but were always glad to share it with them.

If we ever came under attack, these boys would be our only support. As I began to radio the other convoy, Darren and I heard a huge explosion tear through the compound. We grabbed our client and screamed back to the small compound to lock him in a bunker for safety.

As we streaked full blast toward the compound, I radioed for an update from the guards. Some of them were climbing down already in fear. There was a lot of chatter on the radio, and it was clear that the front gate had been hit. Darren and I grabbed all we could, especially my medical gear, and we headed back to the truck.

Leroy, another bearded team contractor jumped in the back with us. We made for the gate, instructing guards as we sped past them. There was a lot of smoke behind the gate when we arrived there. Some 300 meters ahead of it, a British vehicle could be made out in the dark, smoldering and lifeless.

Darren leapt out of the MRAPS vehicle and charged up the top tower to turn on our big flood lights. They did not work. Our generators were not working correctly, and everything was dead. It was dark, and all you could make out was a burning British vehicle. We did not yet know that it was a British convoy of three LAV patrol vehicles that had been coming up one of the smaller dirt roads that swung by our compound.

None of us could tell if the British vehicle was alone or if there were others. We stared helplessly into the dark for a few moments then decided. We would head out there and do what we could for them. My team jumped into the vehicle as Leroy and Darren instructed the guards. We radioed the compound and were out of the gates in seconds. We reached the convoy after a tense, bumpy ride in the dark. As we drew closer we made out two other Brit vehicles speeding in from a short distance away. As we got out, 2 soldiers from the burning vehicle were already trying to wrench open the doors. Flames shot out of the windows, reaching into the darkness and 4 men were screaming inside.

All of us left the vehicle and ran over to help. Darren shouted about security protocol, but no one was listening. The screams of the men inside were too lucid. The vehicle had trundled directly over an IED that had been buried in the road 72 hours before that or less. It burnt from the bottom up, the smoke a darker, more insidious black than the night all around us.

It was hard not to vomit from the smell of burning men. The vehicle was still together somehow but completely compromised inside. The back doors were twisted and would not open. I yelled at the two Brits, asking them if they were okay. They could not hear me; the blast and adrenaline had overcome them.

Their clothes were black and burned, and they had multiple wounds. Blood mixed with soot drenched them from head to foot. The other vehicles had nearly arrived, but the doors would not budge. As the two British vehicles arrived, the familiar spatter of bullets rang out. One of the vehicles immediately turned and fired in their direction. The smell of burning human hair was overwhelming. We all gagged and coughed as we tugged on the doors in all directions. As the British soldiers from the second vehicle leapt from their spot behind us, a lot of shouting ensued. One soldier climbed up the burning LAV, and immediately I realized it must have a top hatch like our MRAPs.

I searched all around the vehicle, but there were no climbing rungs. Suddenly a Brit came falling through the smoke right next to me on the ground. They were pulling the men from the top hatch. More were coming, so I grabbed the half-burning Brit and dragged him away from the LAV by his flack jacket.

Another man fell to the ground, and I dragged him away too. Then another and one more. I told Leroy to wait for the guy who went up there to save them. I began to check them in full medic-mode as Leroy brought the final man to me. I was surrounded by men. Darren was in charge as the platoon leader had been in the burning vehicle.

The two British soldiers from the burning LAV did not think of the hatch on top. They had been in a serious explosion and were lucky to remember their names. A 360-degree perimeter was quickly set up. Radio chatter gurgled into the night. Air support was called as I ran to my truck to grab my medical supplies.

I did everything I could think of to help those men. All four of them were alive but in bad shape. The two from the front had been the driver and vehicle commander. They were not as bad but were quickly whisked away by the other truck. Still a few hundred meters away was the second truck, shooting at an unknown enemy.

I tended to the basics first: triage, trauma, and airway. After about five minutes of tending to these guys, the medic from the other vehicle came running up to me with a lot more gear. I gave him the rundown; he had tended to the other two injured men, and they would be fine, he told me. These men had lots of open wounds, big and small.

One of them was barely breathing, and his airway was closing up. I needed light to drop a new airway in for him. I was told that if I did that, I would have to return to the British base with them. I agreed, and Leroy gave me some light.

Darren and the British army covered our security needs as we worked.

All the while, communications were exchanged back and forth between our compounds. The man I was working on was unconscious, and it took me a few tries to drop the tube. Air support flew overhead, and I felt a little safer. Once all four men had been stabilized for transport, blackened and bleeding, we loaded them into the remaining truck.

I got into the back with the unconscious man that I had just tubed. I had to keep breathing for him during the 20-minute ride back to the British base. We hauled ass back to the small med facility they had inside. I was quickly introduced to the medical staff there and gave them a report on demand. "Good job, Yank," a doctor said to me as I finished.

The team took over, and I stepped outside to calm down. Adrenaline was still rushing in my ears when I tried to slow my breathing by the heli-pad. Darren and Leroy arrived 20 minutes after I did to help me get back to our compound. All of the guys in that blast survived. They were sent out for professional medical treatment that same night.

I heaved myself back into the vehicle, and we sped off out of their gates and into the night, driving fast towards our base. Everyone was silent and alert. We stared into the motionless depths of the dark sky and the stationary mountain landscape. It was a clear, evil feeling, the kind that confirms you are never really safe there.

CHAPTER 11

THE MISSION INSIDE

"War may sometimes be a necessary evil. But no matter how necessary, it is always an evil, never a good. We will not learn how to live together in peace by killing each other's children."

JIMMY CARTER

★ ★  ★ ★

After one solid month of expecting my own death at any moment, I had enjoyed enough of my position with the British company. Joining such a foolhardy group of profiteers had become a discomfort I could no longer stomach. I had to get out, so I did.

The burning soldiers had left something with me, and it did not make my mental state any better. When you are out there fighting the fires, knitting grown men together that have been blown apart by a faceless enemy, the real mission becomes your ability to hold yourself together. Some soldiers do it well. Most of us forget what a quiet mind feels like.

Everything in between becomes an opportunity to eject that pain from inside yourself. It is a valve that constantly needs to be opened so that the steam can escape. And always the violence bubbles beneath the surface. Only men that have stood in the fire of combat can carry this mission inside themselves. It is the mission of every soldier christened by war. With a dead child, the fire grows hotter. A group of burnt men, and still it grows. Each time you adjust. Each time you figure out how to live with what you have experienced. That is why we become dragons in the end. Only a dragon can thrive in the flames of such travesty.

It was later in 2012 I joined a certain company for a more organized (and safer) approach to war. I was never in it to die rich; I was in it to live successfully. Soon I was taken south of Kabul to Ghazni. I would become part of a team that was charged with running high threat security missions in support of the provincial reconstruction of Afghanistan. Wherever a client needed to go, we found a way to get them there.

Our clients would often send us on missions and did not accompany us at all. Certain places were just too dangerous. Whether they came with us or not, we had to go. Our Team Lead could cancel a mission if he thought it was too sketchy, but there had better be a damn good reason for that. Cowardice is feared more than bullets in wartime, so we were always careful to avoid any actions or talk that might indicate fear was the reason we were hesitant.

I was stationed at a Polish Military Base that the U.S. army was sharing in Ghazni. Inside the camp, we had our own small compound. There we ran mobile ground missions that would vary. Sometimes they would take a couple hours, sometimes a couple weeks. We also supported airlift missions when the only safe way to enter an area was by helicopter.

No matter what hell hole we were dropped into, we

managed to make it a livable place. Ghazni was no different. The hooches were small, cramped, and dirty, and the world of war echoed around you through membrane-thin walls as you slept. Here, we lived like prisoners in a system of connected boxes, like jail cells without the bars.

The men were in good spirits at least, and we buddied up to both the Polish and American SF Army personnel, including the EOD teams, pretty quick there. There was always a BBQ on the go, and the outdoor "base-only" boxing matches were fun to watch and participate in to blow off some of that steam. It was not uncommon to see guys sun tanning on the roof of their hooches as helicopters swooped by, including the DragonSlayers, from time to time.

You lived for the time you got to spend among friends, but inevitably, orders would come down. The SF Polish and SF Army units were assigned to support a logistics mission to Khogiyani, a small Afghan army post nestled in a high valley. For 60 days, they had been under siege, and they were in dire need of logistical and firearms support.

If we lost Khogiyani, the Taliban would gain a stronger foothold in the region, a step closer to their overall goal of pushing into the Khost-Gardez passage and surrounding territory. It would increase their strength in the area considerably and would kill any chance that we had to execute further operations in the region. Immediate action was required.

The military decided to support the mission as the logistics being taken to Khogiyani were internally sanctioned. It was our immediate client who recognized the need for additional support due to the location of the Afghan army base and the ever-escalating attacks at this outpost. Strategically, we would be directly involved.

That night, I remember more stars in the sky than I had seen in years. Most nights were clear, with only a faint twinkling of light here and there. It was impossible to keep my eyes closed on that last night. No matter how well we prepared for huge missions like Khogiyani, there was always the "what if." What if this was my last mission? What if I get killed?

My daughter's face was pinned to my consciousness, and it was the only thing that mattered when I closed my eyes. There I was, sleeping in a small, uncomfortable bed, living in a small, uncomfortable hooch, training in a small, uncomfortable Polish army base, and fighting in a big, uncomfortable war. I could have used more rest that night.

My alarm went off that morning and jolted me out of dream-addled oblivion. I hit the community showers extra early to forget. There was something about standing in that hot water that transported you out of that place. I got dressed and loaded up with gear, grabbing my weapons and ammo.

Then I made my way to our MRAP, where Jack and Gary were prepping to mount the 50 cal. So far, working with these men had been seamless. We clicked together like professional soldiers do when they know their place and have the right stones for the job. The morning was darker than night, so each of us had a light clipped to us somewhere. You could get killed at any time on the base, and no one would be able to find you if had no light. We learned that from guys who died in the dark. The military captain we worked with directly was an engineer and a good friend to all of us on the team. He was already at the MRAP, sauntering around the vehicle.

Another engineer who was a civilian, Jeremiah, was also set to come with us. He was a smart guy, perfect for his line of work. Some forty minutes passed, and we headed over to the range to test our fire power. The vehicle mount weapons were always fired before a long mission, so once we knew the 50 cal and machine gun were solid, we joined the SF Polish unit.

They were already staging their vehicles, loaded with logistics and gear. From the moment we landed at their position, it became a nightmare. Just outside of the FOB, on the main road, we knew this was going to be a tough one. By 0600 we headed out, a convoy made up of U.S. and Polish army special forces and both EOD teams.

The mission turned out to be an all day hike, which was unnerving and unpleasant. We took the hard top for 10 to 12 miles then went off road for the rest of the 16-hour trip. I could not believe that Gary sat in his seat and drove the entire way. He was so silent that the rest of us forgot he was even there, doing most of the work.

Gary was always a quiet guy, and we would constantly give him crap about it. I never did shake the feeling that he was sitting there, planning some kind of mass murder-suicide action while we went about our missions. Silence was not an ally in combat, and I paid extra attention to the men that would not engage in the customary ridicule and teasing.

Jack rode in the back of our MRAP, in the forward passenger side seat, so that he could assist the gunner with ammunition when needed. Jeremy, the engineer, rode in the rear passenger seat, and I was in the rear driver's seat. These seating assignments were strategic and chosen for precise reasons.

My medical gear was staged around me, and all the hot coms boxes were to my right. We were a tight fit, and it was stuffy and hot in there. I plugged in our music choice before we left the gate. The beginning of a mission always required excitement, and we were amped to get it going. Usually this lasted throughout the mission, but today's was a drag.

After the first eight hours on the road, boredom threatened to kill us before the Taliban did. We hugged a road that wound through the landscape, leading upwards towards the mountains. Eventually we entered a narrow passage that would take us to Khogiyani. The length of the trip made it hard to stay focused.

We ran out of shit to say to each other after the first few hours melted away. We stopped fucking with each other shortly after that. Soon every man was silent, listening to the radio and trundling towards an outpost that was in desperate need of reinforcements. The Polish EOD team checked the road by foot most of the way.

Before we could drive over it, we had to make sure it was bomb free. Intelligence suggested that it would not be, and we were on a high-risk mission. It was far easier for the Taliban to take us out on the road than to allow us to ever reach Khogiyani. As the Polish team swept and we inched forward, a lull crept over us.

Then they found one. An IED had been buried along the road, waiting to kill. We stopped the convoy, and it took three solid hours for the Polish team to work on the problem. They tried everything they could to detonate or deactivate the device. In the end, exploding it is the easiest option. At least that is what you believe when you are out there.

The Polish EOD team sent their bomb disposal robot at it but could not get the device to budge. It was set in solid ground, so it could not be moved on its own. Then they tried to throw some sort of hook on a rope at it. Eventually, they were just throwing rocks at it to see what would happen. Orders were to not use our MRAP guns unless we had to.

After the first hour, we all wanted to shoot at the thing to blow it up. Each of us had been outside the vehicle at one time or another for two hours, waiting on this progress. Jack had eaten so many MREs already that he was starting to get gassy. And damn him, when he ate a lot of protein, he became the least popular person to be trapped in a MRAP with besides me.

With Jack's continual eating and the stench of stagnancy in the air, we were all ready to move out as soon as possible. Finally, the U.S. Army EOD team pitched up to assist the Polish, and within the hour, we were on our way again. Another four long hours passed before we came to a stop to deal with another IED.

This time it took 40 minutes. We all had consumed a large amount of water on the trip to stay hydrated and alert, which meant bathroom breaks were in desperate need. I had to go really badly that time, and Mike did too. The two of us met up behind the MRAP and took a piss side by side as we fell into familiar teasing patterns.

The captain began to descend from the vehicle turret because he also had to go. I had just been buttoning up the front of my cammie bottoms when we heard the first ping off the side of the MRAP. Mike and I froze and locked eyes as two more bullets flew over our heads and hit our MRAP. Suddenly, the Polish returned fire, directly over our heads.

We were caught in the middle of an all-out shooting match. Instantly, you are ripped out of your lull and thrown into the fire. Your brain comes alive, and adrenaline floods your veins as your body prepares to react to the threat. As bullets hailed over us, Mike said something to me, and I said something back. We had seconds to get out of there, or we would be dead. The two of us made a break for the open back door of the MRAP, nearly mowing the captain down in the process. He had still been clamoring down the vehicle and had not heard the bullets. In the space of two seconds, we began yelling at him to move back up and that we were under attack. Jack reacted fast, grabbing him and forcing him back up the turret.

"Get some! Get some, sir!" he shouted as he pulled the captain upwards. We backed away and ran around the vehicle to the safe side until Jack gave us the all clear. The moment the captain was inside the vehicle, we heard Jack's confirmation. Without a second thought, Mike and I booked it back inside the MRAP.

Mike clamored through the middle of the thing, near the bottom of the turret, where a small opening lay decorated with ammo cans. It was not the usual entrance into the vehicle, but when someone is shooting AK-47 rounds at you, you become a contortionist of note. He jammed himself in that space and squeezed his way inside like human toothpaste.

I jumped in the back and hit the door button to close amidst yells from the rest of the team. "Close the damn door, Doc!" But the doors were eating rounds meant for my face. I adjusted my position and hastily shut the doors just as the captain managed to wind his way back up the turret to return fire.

That was when all hell broke loose. Rounds were being sprayed in every direction, and we had no idea where they were coming from. Surrounded by our armored vehicle, we responded as best we could while the bullets rained down upon the MRAP. The captain shot into space wildly, but none of us knew our enemy's position.

During this extreme moment of panic, Gary remained in his driver's seat wearing his sunglasses and as calm as a gentle breeze. He was waiting for the go ahead from Mike to move out. As the captain fired in all directions, Jack continued to yell at him to "Get some!" urging him to shoot even though we did it blind.

Mike and I heaved and riled from the rush, smiling ear to ear as only you can when you were inches from death. The adrenaline in our bodies caused an outburst of broken laughter before we settled back into the fight. Now, there was a moment we would never forget.

After some gunfire, the Polish Army Mission Commander called in air support. We continued to trade shots for 10 minutes, into the empty wilderness. Every time bullets hit our vehicle, we chose a spot and fired back. Soon, two gunships came screaming over us and lit up the entire set of trees that lay to our east.

After the explosion, all that remained was kindling and a large fire flickering in the distance. The gunshots stopped. The convoy moved out, and jovial chatting started up again. The team traded ideas on how an ambush run by our team would have been far better planned and would have resulted in all of our deaths.

Picking apart a situation that you have just survived is part of the learning process. We did that a lot in combat situations. It was a way to marvel at what you had just overcome and tighten your own skills if the roles were ever reversed. Some two animated hours later, we reached Khogiyani.

The logistics trucks dumped their cargo right next to the small Afghan Army FOB. It was set right in a narrow valley with high mountains all around it. As we approached, it was clear why this outpost was getting nailed so hard. It was, quite frankly, the worst position for an army base any of us had ever seen. Way to give the enemy a fighting chance!

Once we had met with the Polish Mission Commander and his team, we were given two options. The first was that we could stay the night, in which case there was a high probability of attack from all sides. Or we could head back as soon as the cargo was released and see how fast we could hightail it back to our compound.

The road was clear now, and the Taliban would not be able to set another IED in the time it took us to get back if we left soon. After the shooting along the road, we did not have to consider it for very long. When choosing between certain attack and flight to safety, it is the smarter team that chooses safety. We had already dodged the odds that day.

In a matter of minutes, our team decided to drop our load and prepare for the long blitz back to the compound. Every man was worn out from the day and damn near exhausted. But we had no designs on staying in that death trap. Better to leave now and rest with a more realistic shot at safety.

The trip back was fast but debilitating. It took us only three hours to carve our way back through the sandy landscape now that the road had been cleared. The Taliban ambush had failed, and we did not lose anyone that day. But it could have been a different story, and we were never too proud to admit that.

We returned to camp just before it reached 20:00 hours, and we began the routine breakdown of the MRAP. It did not matter how long you were out there; when you got back, you followed protocol. As we were unloading the vehicle, one of the army guys from the Army SF unit stopped by to ask if Jack and I were still interested in the powerlifting competition.

It had been happening that evening, and it was nearly over. We were in time for the tail end. The powerlifting competition would be U.S. personnel against Polish personnel. We had to sign up for the American team as gym rats from each nation faced each other in a test of strength and resilience.

Jack and I had signed up two months before that and had completely forgotten about it. The Khogiyani mission had consumed our thoughts now for weeks. Exhausted from the grueling mission we had just been on, our bodies ached for rest, heat, and a square meal. But we had committed to supporting the American team. And we were still alive yet.

I looked at Jack and immediately knew that he was up for it. "Go ahead and kill yourselves," Mike said as we left with the Army soldier. He would finish up with the vehicles for us. Jack and I changed clothes and were at the gym in ten minutes flat. A lot of people were still milling around, elated by the competition.

Men and women from the Army were competing head to head. We arrived and stepped right into our turn. They had been waiting for us to end off the competition. That day we came off a 20-hour mission where we were nearly toast and walked into a powerlifting competition. As beat as we were, Jack came in second, and I came in third.

My legs were jello, and I ruined the squat, a consequence of the day I imagine. There is no doubt in my mind that we would have won the thing had we not just returned from Khogiyani. But the pair of us were content with our prizes. We had nothing to prove that we did not already prove every day on the job. This was just sauce on a chocolate sundae.

CHAPTER 12
DIVINE PROVIDENCE

"Dragons and legends…It would have been difficult
for any man not to want to fight beside a dragon."
PATRICIA BRIGGS

I took a breath and pulled my mind together. It was so easy to let your life flash in front of you when you felt this close to death. Bullets continued to collide with the rocks and ground all around us. That goddamn QRF team was making my heart pump cold blood. After everything I had been through, to die pinned down in the middle of nowhere?

Mike, Matt, and I were still focused on surviving alone out there in Taliban country. After the powerlifting competition a couple of months ago, and the discovery of the new cannabis strain, it would be such a joke to have it end here in the dirt. Your mind does anything it can to get through that kind of trauma.

You see the turning points in your life, the moments when decisions brought you to where you are now. We had been looking to find the best spot for a new base and had wound up in the throes of an ambush. Only, this time, we had no back up, and all that stood between us was the unforgiving landscape against native-born killers.

I clung to the hope that finding that strain was divine providence and that I would not die on my own in the desert that day. I was full of purpose now that the fates had shown me my future. I would take the strain back to America, grow it, and test it. I would be instrumental in curing PTSD for every person that had ever stood in the fire. For every dragon.

This thought kept me pinned to that rock, hugging it for dear life. When the Quick Reaction Force finally came and laid down some heavy fire, it was an hour later than it should have been, something about a delay at the base. Jack sped up to us afterwards, and we piled into the MRAP, frazzled from the emotional experience of being caught in the open under gunfire.

The trip back to the base was sobering. Instead of dwelling on the past, I could focus on the future. Mike, Matt, and I all knew that we had cheated death on this mission. However, any security we felt was only momentary, and nowhere within these borders was truly safe for any of us. We were there to work, to shoot, to save, and to kill. We were contractors, and we were soldiers.

The days stretched out before us, and my resolve hardened. I fashioned a plan to move my medical cannabis seeds around with me in relative safety, knowing that locked inside each of them were the genetics I needed to preserve. I knew that the strain was rare and that it obliterated my PTSD symptoms.

More research needed to be done, and I was the man to do it. By 2013 we had been in Ghazni for two weeks, we were winding down and demobilizing operations there. The Kabul PRT teams were hit hard by suicide bombers, and they were immediately flown to Ghazni for medical attention.

The Taliban[9] openly claimed credit for the attack that killed three coalition soldiers and two civilian personnel who worked for the Kabul Provincial Reconstruction Team. Their convoy was struck as it traveled to a school, and there were a lot of serious injuries.

As usual, the Taliban reported that a lot more people were killed than genuinely were in an effort to make themselves seem effective. When I had arrived on base, I entered the Ghazni Aid Station and introduced myself to the medical staff, giving them my contact details in case they ever needed any additional help with medical emergencies.

At my skill level, I was a talented physician's assistant, and in an emergency situation, I could triage with the best of them. The front door to the Aid Station was perhaps a one-minute jog from my hooch. On that day, I was so close that I heard the bird land and a second one behind it. We all knew something had happened.

I was hanging out of my hooch by the time the third bird had landed on the strip. Three helicopters full of injured people? I darted out of my hooch and sprinted over to the aid station to be of service. The helo medics were bringing in the wounded and giving their reports as I arrived.

Each of the medical staff were working at high speed, and it was clear that there were not enough doctors to go around. So I jumped right in after hesitating for a few seconds. I

---

9   Bill Roggio, Taliban Suicide Bomber Kills 5 ISAF Personnel In Southeastern Afghanistan, http://www.longwarjournal.org/archives/2013/04/taliban_suicide_bomb_46.

helped move a soldier to a bed in the ER; he seemed stable, but there was blood everywhere.

There must have been 50 people in that ER room clamoring to help the wounded. I took a good look at the soldier's injuries, and both of his legs had been blown to bits. His left foot was missing, and his right foot was barely hanging on. He floated in and out of consciousness, alternating from adrenaline to overwhelming shock.

I tried talking to him as calmly as I could as I was working. He mumbled a lot, and I could barely hear him amidst the noise. At one point, I believe he was asking me about his team and who was hurt. Then he passed out.

As I looked up, a doctor settled at his feet and began examining them. I was asked to hold his right foot in place as it was examined. The tourniquets in place controlled the bleeding well, but it was not enough. I locked eyes with the doctor, and he said, "It has to come off." Another nurse was called over to help take over holding the man's legs in place.

The doctor was pulled to another patient. Before he left, he said, "Remove the rest of the foot, keep the bleeding controlled, and pack him up for transport." I did not think. I just did. It all happened in the space of 20 minutes. Once stabilized and ready, all of the injured were flown out. I found my way back to my hooch, pulling off my blood-soaked clothes.

I sat there in my room, covered in that man's blood, and put on some music. It was a while before I was calm enough to take a shower.

By May of 2013 we were tasked with a mission for Intel on an area at Zarghun Shar. When we were about two thirds of the way there, two RPGs were fired at us one after the other. The first RPG hit 20 meters away from our convoy; the other hit 50 meters away.

As the RPGs exploded out of range, small arms fire broke out. The mission was a bust, and we had no choice but to turn back and head for cover. We hauled ass back to the compound, taking a different route to get there. In our haste, we came upon a wadi that was quite flooded with fast-flowing water.

When the mountains of the region start to thaw, the rivers created by all of that melted snow are something to see. Just incredible. It is no wonder the valley becomes so lush and green. The enemy could have been closing in behind us, so we made the decision to cross the wadi then and there, despite the risk.

At the time, there were several other cars and locals that had stopped there due to the flood, and we had no idea who was friendly and who was not. We had to take a chance. With our principal in the back seat, it was our job to get him to safety. He did not say a single word until we got back inside the compound.

Mike went through first as Matt drove, and they made it look easy, so we followed. Then their heavy up-armored vehicle began to slip sideways in the rushing water. A few more feet and they would plummet off the edge into a huge river. They dug in deep as we also started to slip and powered on.

We were in the middle of the wadi when I yelled to Jack to move it. He kept his eyes fixed on the bank and drove hard. We made it through, booked back to the KKG compound, and counted four brand new bullet holes in both of our vehicles. That was a close call, and we laughed about it afterwards. What else was there to do?

Then the end came. It came suddenly, as it does, and it took me out of the war. It was a simple routine security escort on foot that did it. As the team and I were jumping over a large ditch, the rock that I had placed my right foot on gave way, and I fell backwards, twisting my whole body because of the heavy kit and the weight from my weapon.

I dropped five to six feet down into a narrow space and was trapped between two walls. Once my team was able to fish me out of there, the extent of my injuries became clearer. I knew that on impact I had damaged something in my back, but when I tried to straighten out, my neck protested in severe pain.

I was already set for rotation home in June, and now I found myself injured. I made it back to the compound in one pain-streaked piece and sauntered over to the tiny aid station at KKG. As suspected, they could do no more for me. I just had to be careful and let things heal.

For about three days I lay in my hooch, unable to stand up. I had to crawl to the bathroom, which was extremely painful. Every cough or sneeze felt like knives severing my spinal cord. My lower back and neck were not happy. I could barely move without the pain tearing at me like nails on raw skin.

I decided to be my own medic, so I treated myself and compiled my own reports. The medication helped some, and soon I found that I could carry myself upright again. I hated being hurt because it let my team down. I gradually healed and was able to go on a few minor missions again before rotating out of the war forever. Then June came and an emotional goodbye. I had thought long and hard about it and decided that it would be my last tour. I had the strain I needed, the one I was meant to find and a real purpose back in the U.S. Inside, I was happy knowing that the strain I carried would end the war for me on a personal level in a way I had never experienced before.

Even more exciting was the opportunity to bring this PTSD cure to so many people that needed it: the men at home that could no longer stifle their anger over what they had seen and done and the women unable to have kids because of the pain of combat. So many problems could be solved with this miracle plant, so many lives saved.

Sometimes I wonder if I had discovered this strain before Brian died whether it might have saved his life. No one ever died from medical marijuana. I said goodbye to Mike, Matt, and Jack, along with many of the other guys I had fought alongside in those final days. I boarded the helicopter and left that place, glad to leave it behind.

Almost an hour later, Afghan soldiers opened fire on U.S. troops right next door at the Afghan National Army Base, killing two U.S. soldiers and a civilian while wounding three other Americans. Mike told me all about it; he and Jack were the first on the scene. Mike called it a blood bath. They did what they could until more help arrived from the Army. Everyone was DOA.

Later on the telephone, Mike told me that all he could think was how typical it was. *Just as Gage leaves this fucking place*, he thought to himself. In war, there is never a good time to arrive or leave. From the moment you are there, you are in danger and your life no longer belongs to you. You are part of a team, and that team keeps you alive.

TF Dragon Slayer was an important team to me. Fighting with them and discovering the strain in the Hindu Kush were among the most meaningful times of my life. I managed to smuggle the seeds back home without much trouble, although I did get hung up by Homeland Security as they randomly picked me for a search while transferring through Atlanta. That was a close call. The entire time a sense of calm stayed with me, like I knew I was doing the right thing and would not be caught.

When I arrived back in the U.S., my life took on new meaning. I thought about the day I discovered those seeds and the nightmare I had to wade through to get them back home. A series of unlikely events made it possible for me to begin my research. It has become a passion of mine and will remain so until I get the word out about it. These little seeds were tucked away in a plant growing in the middle of winter, 7,500 to 8,000 feet above sea level, in torturous weather extremes. Their existence was a miracle before I stumbled across them; imagine what they could do for mankind. It was never my intention to just "grow some weed" that I found during the war. All of the risk I have taken I have done for a reason very close to my heart. I have gone through a lot since coming home. I have lost my marriage and nearly everything I own, and I have been forced to move away from my daughter, who I came home to be with. I even quit a professional job that I excelled at to focus on this passion. I believe that this strain holds the key for combat veterans. I was young once and full of dreams about life. I saw war as a means to an end. But war has no end for the people that get caught up in it. That is why so many good people can never return to the lives they had before. Once you allow that kind of pain into your life, it never goes away.

And then the cycle begins. Doctors. Lawyers. Diagnosis. Bipolar disorder, PTSD, anxiety, attention deficit, explosive moments, and more. They put you on medication that switches off your body and dilutes your brain. You fight. You tear your life apart. All the while, the war inside you rages on. No amount of alcohol exists that can dull the pain of it. You are forced inside that place whenever your eyes flutter closed.

War is unlikely to change. But I do not believe that good men and women have to carry it with them anymore. There is a need for the development of this strain into an adequate cure for PTSD. Imagine a world where our fighters come back home and the fight stops. Mothers can be mothers again. Husbands and wives can return to loving families. Someone's father is able to hold down a job and even excel at it. These are the dreams that consume me now, since the day I stood on top of that mountain. I believe that this Kush is the answer to it all, a replacement for the medications that make it impossible for them to function.

I have been taking beatings since I was a kid. The worst beatings I ever took were the ones I inflicted on myself because of PTSD. It is a sweeping and brutal disorder for every veteran that I have ever met. These people have suffered enough. They do not deserve to return home to ruin, abandonment, and poverty. But that is what they get.

I am home now, and my combat days are over. I will never stop being a soldier, and I will never stop being a medic. The brotherhood never dies. And to this end, I want to dedicate my future. I am here to shout it across the world. There is hope for PTSD, and there is hope for veterans like me! Medical marijuana can give you your life back. It gave me mine.

Will you join me in letting every soldier know? Your hope lies in a tiny seed. If you or anyone you know suffers from post-traumatic stress disorder, I strongly urge you to test the war strain for yourself. Donate to the development of this cure, and stand beside me as the horrors of our past disappear in a cloud of smoke.

CONCLUSION

My name is Robert Floyd Amsler Junior, but you can call me Gage. My men call me "Doc." I have been a paramedic, a fire fighter, a highly trained combat medic, and a security protection specialist contractor working in war zones throughout the Kuwait, Iraq, and Afghanistan conflicts.

I have lost friends in these battles and pieces of myself along the way. Once war was a life plan for me, a way I could support my family, study, and create my own American dream. But the dream turned out to be a nightmare when I got back home.

PTSD and instability robbed me of my life, my family, and my future. I was called back into the arms of war again and again, with nowhere else to turn. Then I found it. The strain of Hindu Kush in an impossible location, untouched by human interference. On smoking it, I discovered an instant and longer-lasting relief from my PTSD than any medication I had ever been prescribed before. I believe it is a cure—a sustainable, natural cure that the government should be prescribing to every combat veteran with PTSD.

It has become my mission to tell the world about this strain. Now that you have read my story and have joined me on the long journey to this point, you understand. There is real importance here for our men and women on the ground.

Let's join forces and make my war strain widely available to everyone that needs it. Let's get the funding required for additional research into PTSD and treating it with this strain. It takes a team to make it through war. Now I need a new kind of team—one that will help me bring this cure to soldiers that have lost it all and want it back.

My life is better now. I live with a quiet mind and a relaxed heart. When I feel the war threaten to overcome me, all I have to do is stop and take a deep breath. No side effects. No anger. No nausea or pain. Just understanding and the peace that comes with a stable mind.

This is my war strain. This is our future.

- R. GAGE AMSLER

CONCLUSION

Chapter 1

Bill Hicks, ThinkExist, http://thinkexist.com/quotation/why_is_marijuana_against_the_law-it_grows/330565.html

Chapter 2

Christensen, Jen, *10 Diseases Where Medical Marijuana Could Have An Impact*, http://edition.cnn.com/2015/04/15/health/marijuana-medical-advances/

Chapter 3

Top 10 Marijuana Quotes EVER, http://michiganweed.org/top-10-marijuana-quotes-ever/

Chapter 4

How Did Marijuana Become Illegal In The First Place? http://www.drugpolicy.org/blog/how-did-marijuana-become-illegal-first-place

Post-Traumatic Stress Disorder (PTSD), http://www.helpguide.org/articles/ptsd-trauma/post-traumatic-stress-disorder.htm

Chapter 5

Cannabis Quotes, http://www.dailysmoker.com/various/cannabis-quotes

Chapter 6

Gupta, Sinjay, Dr, *Dr Sinjay Gupta's Top 10 Quotes On Marijuana*, http://www.leafscience.com/2013/09/26/dr-sanjay-guptas-top-10-quotes-marijuana/

Barclay, Sam, R, *The Science Of Medical Marijuana: What's The Latest?* http://www.healthline.com/health-news/latest-science-of-medical-marijuana-022115

Lee, Martin, A, *The Discovery Of The Endocannabinoid System*, http://www.beyondthc.com/wp-content/uploads/2012/07/eCBSystemLee.pdf

Chapter 7

War Quotes, http://www.brainyquote.com/quotes/topics/topic_war.html

Chapter 8

War Quotes, http://www.brainyquote.com/quotes/topics/topic_war.html

Chapter 9

War Quotes, http://www.brainyquote.com/quotes/topics/topic_war.html

Chapter 10

Top Ten Quotes On PTSD, https://annarosemeeds.wordpress.com/2014/06/24/top-ten-quotes-on-ptsd

Chapter 11

War Quotes, http://www.notable-quotes.com/w/war_quotes.html

Chapter 12

Quotes About Dragon, http://www.goodreads.com/quotes/tag/dragon

Roggio, Bill, *Taliban Suicide Bomber Kills 5 ISAF Personnel In Southeastern Afghanistan*, http://www.longwarjournal.org/archives/2013/04/taliban_suicide_bomb_46.php

Made in the USA
San Bernardino, CA
27 March 2016